Introduction

This revision guide is matched to the new Edexcel GCSE Mathematics linear specification (2540). As such, it provides full coverage of everything that might be tested in the two terminal exam papers. Just as importantly, it contains no superfluous material, which means you won't waste any of your time revising material that isn't relevant.

This guide is also suitable for use by students following the modular specification (2544). To help these students, the contents list (page 3) includes module numbers for easy referencing.

The material in this guide is tailored to the needs of Foundation Tier students. It is divided into four sections: Number; Algebra; Shape, Space and Measures; and Handling Data, to help you focus and develop your skills. Information is presented in a user-friendly format, with clear, easy to follow explanations and exam-style examples.

Ideally this guide should be used with the companion workbook (contact our customer services department for details), which will allow you to practise your skills, reinforcing your understanding of the material covered. The workbook matches the revision guide page for page and consists of structured questions with spaces for answers, plus extension questions.

Please note, a separate revision guide and workbook are available for Higher Tier students.

Consultant Editor: John Proctor

A respected Education Consultant with over 14 years teaching experience, John Proctor is an expert in mathematics and ICT education. He is the former Director of Specialist College, St. Mary's Catholic School in Astley.

Contributor: Tina Foster

Formerly the Head of Mathematics at a large comprehensive school, Tina Foster is now employed as a Mathematics Consultant by a local authority and has an excellent understanding of the new two-tier specification, which she is helping to implement in local schools.

ISBN: 1-905129-77-7

Published by Lonsdale, A division of Huveaux Plc

Consultant Editor: John Proctor
Project Editor: Rebecca Skinner
Cover and Concept Design: Sarah Duxbury

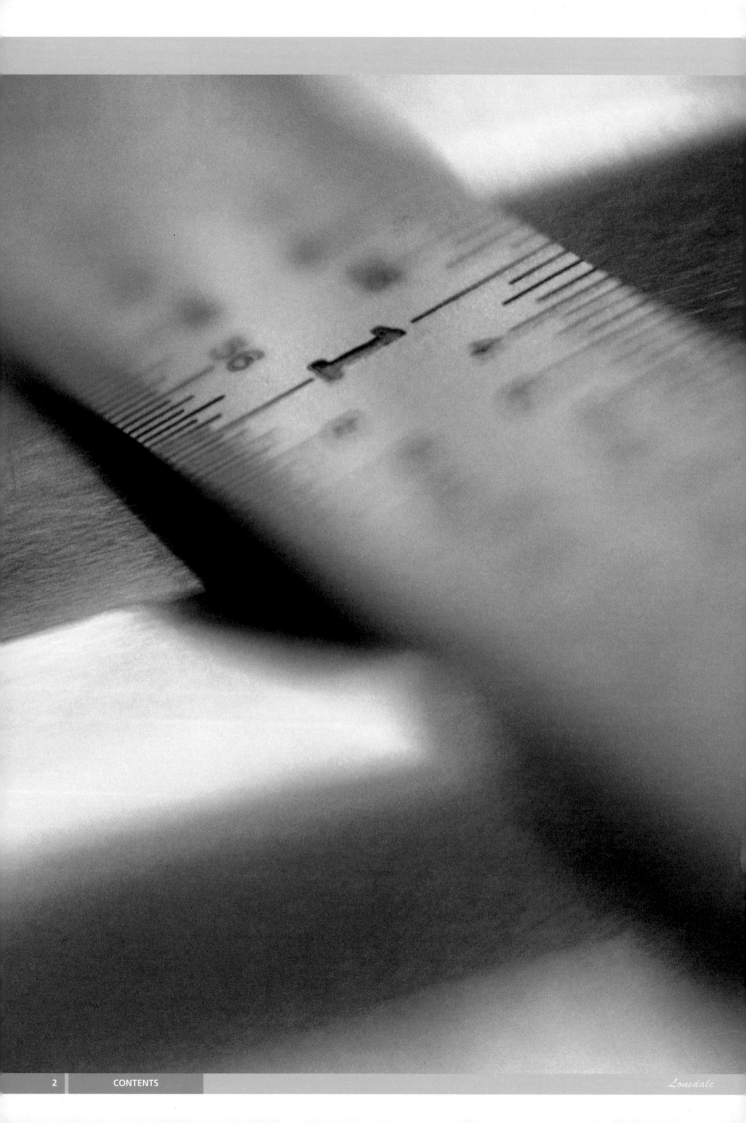

Lonsdale

Contents

Number

Algebra

Shape, Space & Measures

Handling Data

If you are following the modular specification (2544), the numbers in brackets indicate which unit(s) the content of each page is relevant to.

Place Value

Place Value in Whole Numbers

The value of a digit in a whole number depends on its position in the number. This is called its place value (see the table below). The table below can easily be extended to include ten thousands, hundred thousands, millions etc. This means that it does not matter how large a number is, each digit will still have a place value.

Place Value of Digits				Number
1000 Thousands	**100** Hundreds	**10** Tens	**1** Units	
			7	Seven
		4	2	Forty two
	6	5	9	Six hundred and fifty nine
3	1	8	5	Three thousand, one hundred and eighty five

· ·

Rounding Numbers

Numbers can be very large and often these numbers make more sense if they are rounded to a given power of 10 e.g. 10 (10^1), 100 (10^2), 1000 (10^3). Let's take the attendance at a football match. The actual attendance is 38 726. However to a neutral observer an attendance figure to the nearest thousand would have more meaning. Look at the place value table below which shows this attendance.

The digit to the right of the one you are working to will tell you if you need to round up. For example, when rounding a number to the nearest thousand you need to look at the digit in the hundreds column. If it is 5 or more, the digit in the thousands column is **rounded up**. If it is 4 or less the digit in the thousands column **stays the same**. The digits in the hundreds, tens and units columns become zero, showing the number to the nearest 1000.

10 000 Ten Thousands	**1000** Thousands	**100** Hundreds	**10** Tens	**1** Units
3	9	0	0	0
3	8	7	0	0
3	8	7	3	0
3	8	7	2	6

Nearest 1000: Round up

Nearest 100: Stays the same

Nearest 10: Round up

Numbers 1

Types of Number

Numbers can be described in many ways. Below is a summary of the types of number that you should know.

Even Numbers

These are numbers which can be divided exactly by 2. The first ten even numbers in order are…

2, 4, 6, 8, 10, 12, 14, 16, 18, 20

Odd Numbers

Since all whole numbers are either even or odd then odd numbers are those that cannot be divided exactly by 2. The first ten odd numbers in order are…

1, 3, 5, 7, 9, 11, 13, 15, 17, 19

Factors

The factors of a number are those whole numbers which divide exactly into it. All numbers, with the exception of square numbers (see page 14), have an even number of factors. An easy way to find the factors of a number is to choose pairs of numbers that multiply to give that number. For example…

The factors of **10** are **1, 2, 5, 10**
(since 1 x 10 = 10, 2 x 5 =10)
The factors of **24** are **1, 2, 3, 4, 6, 8, 12, 24**
(since 1 x 24 = 24, 2 x 12 =24, 3 x 8 = 24, 4 x 6 = 24)

As we said, square numbers have an odd number of factors, for example…

The factors of **16** are **1, 2, 4, 8, 16**
(since 1 x 16 = 16, 2 x 8 =16, 4 x 4 = 16)
The factors of **36** are
1, 2, 3, 4, 6, 9, 12, 18, 36
(since 1 x 36 = 36, 2 x 18 = 36,
3 x 12 = 36, 4 x 9 = 36, 6 x 6 = 36)

Multiples

The multiples of a number are those numbers which can be divided exactly by it. To put it simply, they are the numbers found in the 'times' tables.

The multiples of **5** are **5, 10, 15, 20, 25** and so on…

The multiples of **8** are **8, 16, 24, 32, 40** and so on…

Prime Numbers

These are numbers which have only two factors: **1** and **the number itself**. The first ten prime numbers are…

2, 3, 5, 7, 11, 13, 17, 19, 23, 29

The only even prime number is 2 since all even numbers after this have 2 as a factor, which rules them out as prime numbers.

Reciprocals

The reciprocal of a number is simply '1 over that number', for example…

- the reciprocal of 4 is '1 over 4' = $\frac{1}{4}$

- the reciprocal of 0.2 is '1 over 0.2'

$= \frac{1}{0.2} = \frac{10}{2} = 5$

- the reciprocal of $\frac{2}{3}$ is '1 over $\frac{2}{3}$'

$= \frac{1}{\frac{2}{3}} = 1 \div \frac{2}{3} = 1 \times \frac{3}{2} = \frac{3}{2} = 1\frac{1}{2}$

Any non-zero number multiplied by its reciprocal is always equal to 1, for example…

$= 4 \times \frac{1}{4} = 1$, $0.2 \times 5 = 1$, $\frac{2}{3} \times \frac{3}{2} = 1$

Also, zero has no reciprocal because division by zero results in infinity.

Numbers 2

Prime Factor Form

The prime factors of a number are those prime numbers which divide exactly into it. When a number is expressed as a product of its prime factors it is said to be written in prime factor form. All you have to do is divide your number by the lowest prime number and then keep repeating until it will not divide exactly. You then try the next prime number up etc. until you end up with an answer of 1.

Examples...

1 Write **24** in prime factor form.

```
2 | 24
2 | 12
2 | 6
3 | 3
    1
```

so $24 = 2 \times 2 \times 2 \times 3 = 2^3 \times 3$

2 Write **90** in prime factor form.

```
2 | 90
3 | 45
3 | 15
5 | 5
    1
```

so $90 = 2 \times 3 \times 3 \times 5 = 2 \times 3^2 \times 5$

Alternatively a prime factor tree can be used to work out the prime factors of a number. Take 24 as our example again:

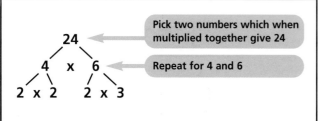

Pick two numbers which when multiplied together give 24

Repeat for 4 and 6

2 x 2 x 2 x 3 is the prime factor form of 24

Highest Common Factor (HCF)

The highest common factor of two (or more) numbers is the highest factor that divides exactly into both (or all of) the numbers. To find the HCF express your numbers in prime factor form and then select only the prime factors that are common.

Example...

What is the HCF of **24** and **90**?

Firstly express **24** and **90** in prime factor form...

$24 = 2 \times 2 \times \boxed{2 \times 3}$
$90 = \boxed{2 \times 3} \times 3 \times 5$

... and then select prime factors that are common to both numbers.

HCF of 24 and 90 = 2 x 3 = 6

Lowest (Least) Common Multiple (LCM)

The lowest (or least) common multiple of two (or more) numbers is the lowest number that is a multiple of both (or all of) the numbers. To find the LCM write down the first ten multiples of each number and then select the lowest multiple that is common.

Example...

What is the LCM of **8** and **10**?

Write down the multiples of each number...

The multiples of **8** are: **8, 16, 24, 32, ㊵, 48, 56, 64, 72, 80 and so on...**
The multiples of **10** are: **10, 20, 30, ㊵, 50, 60, 70, 80, 90, 100 and so on...**

... and then select the lowest multiple that is common.

LCM of 8 and 10 is 40
(From the two lists above, 80 is also a multiple that is common. However it is NOT the lowest).

Addition and Subtraction of Whole Numbers

Whenever you add or subtract whole numbers you must line up the digits, one on top of the other, in place value order.

Examples...

1 356 + 72

$$
\begin{array}{r}
356 \\
+ \ {}_1 72 \\
\hline
428
\end{array}
$$

- Start from the right hand side.
- **6 + 2 = 8**. Put **8** down.
- **5 + 7 = 12**. Put **2** down and carry **1**.
- **3 + 1 = 4**. Put **4** down.

2 438 - 57

$$
\begin{array}{r}
{}^3\cancel{4}{}^1 38 \\
- \ \ \ 57 \\
\hline
381
\end{array}
$$

- Start from the right hand side.
- **8 - 7 = 1**. Put **1** down.
- **3 - 5** doesn't work. Borrow 1 from the hundreds column to give **13 - 5 = 8**. Put **8** down.
- **3 - 0 = 3**. Put **3** down.

Multiplication and Division of Whole Numbers by Powers of 10

To multiply a whole number by a power of 10, e.g. $10(10^1)$, $100(10^2)$, $1000(10^3)$, all you have to do is move all the digits a certain number of place values to the left, as determined by the power. When you do this your number becomes bigger, for example...

1 $36 \times 10 = 360$

2 $36 \times 100 = 3600$

3 $36 \times 1000 = 36\,000$

To divide a whole number by a power of 10 you move all the digits a certain number of places to the right, as determined by the power. When you do this your number becomes smaller, for example...

1 $36 \div 10 = 3.6$

2 $36 \div 100 = 0.36$

3 $36 \div 1000 = 0.036$

Long Multiplication and Long Division of Whole Numbers

To be successful at long multiplication and long division you need to know the multiplication or 'times' tables.

Examples...

1 364 x 14

$$
\begin{array}{r}
364 \\
\times \ 14 \\
\hline
3640 \\
1\,{}^2 4 {}^1 56 \\
\hline
5096
\end{array}
$$

- **14 = 10 + 4**.
- Do the **364 x 10** first. Remember to put a '**0**' down as you would if you multiplied any whole number by **10**.
- Do the **364 x 4** multiplication.
- Add the two multiplications together.

2 312 ÷ 12

$$
\begin{array}{r}
26 \\
12\overline{)312} \\
24\downarrow \\
\hline
72 \\
72 \\
\hline
0
\end{array}
$$

- **12** does not divide into **3** so move on.
- **12** into **31** goes **2** times. **12 x 2 = 24**. Write **24** below **31** and subtract to give **7**.
- Bring down the **2**. **12** into **72** goes **6** times. **12 x 6 = 72**.

Integers 1

What are Integers?

Integers are all the whole numbers which are greater than zero, less than zero, and zero itself. Above zero the numbers are positive although we don't write a + (plus) in front of them. Below zero the numbers are negative and these must have a - (minus) written in front of them. When you use positive and negative numbers, zero is the fixed point on the scale. All numbers relate to this point.

A number scale (which can be horizontal or vertical) can be a very useful aid for you to understand positive and negative numbers.

Positive and negative numbers are often used in everyday life, e.g. to show temperatures above and below freezing or financial gain and loss.

A number scale

A Bank Statement showing deposits and withdrawals.

LONSDALE BUILDING SOCIETY

Date	Description	Deposit	Withdrawal	Balance
11/12/03				£226.30
12/12/03	The Toy Shop		-£49.99	£176.31
13/12/03	Gas Bill		-£21.03	£155.28
14/12/03	Cheque	£25.00		£180.28
16/12/03	La Trattoria		-£32.98	£147.30
19/12/03	Rent		-£260.00	-£112.70

Ordering Integers

This means rearranging a series of positive and negative numbers in either ascending (lowest to highest) or descending (highest to lowest) order.

The simplest way is to collect all the negative and positive numbers together in two separate groups. If need be you can then use a number scale to order the numbers.

Example

Rearrange the following temperatures in ascending order:
7°C, -1°C, 2°C, 5°C, -4°C, -2°C, 3°C, -8°C

Collect the negative and positive numbers together in two separate groups and order using a number scale...

... to give us the temperatures in ascending order: **-8°C, -4°C, -2°C, -1°C, 2°C, 3°C, 5°C, 7°C**

Addition & Subtraction of Integers

When you are adding or subtracting integers always draw a number scale to help you. Positive numbers are counted to the right of the number scale and negative numbers to the left.

> ### Examples...
>
> **1** At 6pm the temperature in Manchester was 6°C. By 10pm it had fallen by 8°C. The temperature at 10pm is therefore **6°C - 8°C**. On a number scale this calculation can be shown by starting at 6 and then counting 8 to the left...
>
>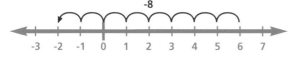
>
> ... **6°C - 8°C = -2°C**
>
> **2** The temperature had fallen a further 6°C by 1am. On a number scale this can be shown by starting at -2 and counting 6 places to the left...
>
>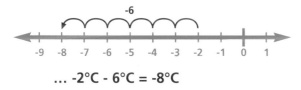
>
> ... **-2°C - 6°C = -8°C**

Manchester
6°C

Multiplication & Division of Integers

When you are multiplying or dividing integers ignore any signs and multiply or divide the two numbers to get the number part of the answer. If the numbers have **like** signs the answer is **positive**, whereas if the numbers have **different** signs the answer is **negative**. This table shows all the possibilities:

Examples...

1 6 x -7 = -42

2 -12 x 8 = -96

3 -11 x -5 = 55

4 75 ÷ -5 = -15

5 -200 ÷ 40 = -5

6 -99 ÷ -11 = 9

Multiplication of Integers	+ X + = +
	- X - = +
	+ X - = -
	- X + = -
Division of Integers	+ ÷ + = +
	- ÷ - = +
	+ ÷ - = -
	- ÷ + = -

Order of Operations

Bidmas

The simplest possible calculation involves only one operation, e.g. an addition or multiplication, which is easy enough to work out.

However, when a calculation involves more than one operation, you must carry them out in the order shown here.

B I D M A S

| BRACKETS | INDICES (OR POWERS) | DIVISIONS AND MULTIPLICATIONS - THESE CAN BE DONE IN ANY ORDER | ADDITIONS AND SUBTRACTIONS - AGAIN IN ANY ORDER |

Examples...

1 8 + 3 x 4

Do the multiplication first

= 8 + 12

Then the addition

= 20

2 $\dfrac{(14 + 6)}{-4}$

Do the addition in the bracket first

= $\dfrac{20}{-4}$

Then the division

= -5 (+ ÷ - = -)

3 4^2 - 2 x 5

Work out the square first

= 16 - 2 x 5

Then the multiplication

= 16 - 10

Then the subtraction

= 6

Work through these examples again, only this time do the operations in the wrong order. You should get different answers which are wrong!

Use of Brackets

The insertion of a bracket (or brackets) into a calculation can drastically change the final answer.

Do remember that if you are asked to insert a bracket into a calculation that involves more than one operation there is always more than one possibility. Make sure that you try out all the different possibilities.

Example...

Here is a calculation with no brackets in it.

8 + 3 x 4 - 2 = 8 + 12 - 2 = 20 - 2 = 18
(or 8 + 10)

If we now insert one bracket into the calculation the possible answers become...

(8 + 3) x 4 - 2 = 11 x 4 - 2 = 44 - 2 = 42

8 + 3 x (4 - 2) = 8 + 3 x 2 = 8 + 6 = 14

Previously on page 4 we have rounded very large numbers to a given power of 10. We will now go a couple of stages further and round numbers to a given number of Decimal Places and Significant Figures.

Rounding a Number to 1 Decimal Place

These are numbers that are only allowed one digit after the decimal point. To round a number to 1 decimal place (1 d.p.) we must look at the **second** digit after the decimal point. There are two possibilities:

If the second digit after the decimal point is **4 or less** (i.e. 0, 1, 2, 3 or 4) we leave the first digit after the decimal point as it is.

Examples...

1. **7.43** to 1 d.p. is **7.4**.

2. **167.14** to 1 d.p. is **167.1**.

If the second digit after the decimal point is **5 or more** (i.e. 5, 6, 7, 8 or 9) we **round up** and add 1 to the first digit after the decimal point.

Examples...

1. **7.48** to 1 d.p. is **7.5**.

2. **53.7503** to 1 d.p. is **53.8**.

Rounding a Number to 2 or more Decimal Places

To round a number to 2 d.p. we are only allowed two digits after the decimal point. This time we must look at the **third** digit after the decimal point to decide whether we need to round up or to keep the second digit after the decimal point the same.

To round a number to 3 d.p. we must look at the **fourth** digit and so on. Unless a question tells you otherwise, always give money to 2 decimal places. Amounts of money are rounded to 2 d.p. in exactly the same way as below.

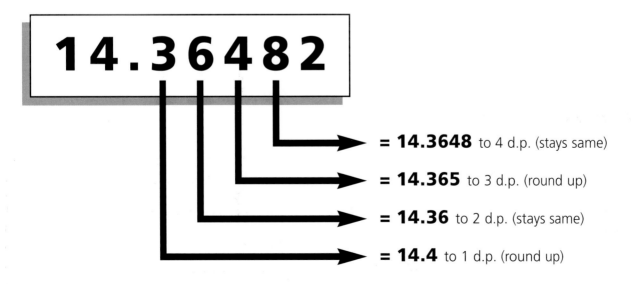

14.36482

= **14.3648** to 4 d.p. (stays same)

= **14.365** to 3 d.p. (round up)

= **14.36** to 2 d.p. (stays same)

= **14.4** to 1 d.p. (round up)

Rounding Numbers 2

Significant Figures for Numbers Greater Than 1

Rounding a number to a certain number of significant figures (s.f.) is very like rounding a number to a certain number of decimal places.

To round a number to 1 s.f. we need to look at the second digit and round up or leave the same. To round a number to 2 s.f. we need to look at the third digit and so on.

The number alongside is the attendance at a pop concert. It has 4 significant figures.

1st s.f. 2nd s.f. 3rd s.f. 4th s.f.

6 8 2 5

7000 to 1 s.f. (round up)

6800 to 2 s.f. (stays same)

6830 to 3 s.f. (round up)

Another Example...

130.71

to 4 s.f. is **130.7**
to 3 s.f. is **131**
to 2 s.f. is **130**
to 1 s.f. is **100**

NOTE:
130.71 has 5 significant figures. The 0 (zero) **does** count as it is in between digits.

Significant Figures for Numbers Less Than 1

These follow the same rules except we start counting our significant figures from the first digit greater than 0 (zero). For example...

0.00007 = 1SF

1st s.f. 2nd s.f. 3rd s.f. 4th s.f.

0.03617

0.04 to 1 s.f. (round up)

0.036 to 2 s.f. (stays same)

0.0362 to 3 s.f. (round up)

Estimating and Checking

Estimating Answers

The answer to many calculations can be estimated by rounding numbers within the calculations to 1 significant figure.

Examples...

Estimate the answers to the following calculations:

1   71 + 18 - 26

$\cong$ 70 + 20 - 30

= 60 (Actual answer is 63)

2 $\dfrac{43 \times 2.9}{61.34}$

$\cong \dfrac{40 \times 3}{60}$

$= \dfrac{120}{60}$

= 2 (Actual answer is 2.03 (2 d.p.))

3 $\dfrac{3.6 \times 10.4}{7.7 - 3.1}$

$\cong \dfrac{4 \times 10}{8 - 3}$

$= \dfrac{40}{5}$

= 8 (Actual answer is 8.14 (2 d.p.))

4 $\dfrac{413 \times 4.87}{0.189}$

$\cong \dfrac{400 \times 5}{0.2}$

$= \dfrac{2000}{0.2}$

= 10 000
(Actual answer is 10 600 (3 s.f.))

Checking your Answers for Accuracy

Answers to calculations can be checked for accuracy by starting with your answer and working backwards, reversing the maths.

Examples...

1   8 x 7 = 56 ⟶ $\dfrac{56}{8} = 7$ ✓ or $\dfrac{56}{7} = 8$ ✓

2

The table below shows the amount of money collected by a small local charity from October to December, using collecting tins at three different locations. Check it for accuracy.

MONTH	Location 1	Location 2	Location 3	TOTAL
Oct	28.08	16.73	18.23	63.04
Nov	32.96	21.01	18.16	72.13
Dec	26.12	19.57	16.03	61.72
TOTAL	87.16	57.31	52.42	**196.89**

For this example, there are several ways of checking it for accuracy. You could check the totals for each month (rows) or the totals for each location (columns). Finally, check the overall total.

- 63.04 + 72.13 + 61.72 = 196.89
  196.89 - 61.72 - 72.13 = 63.04 ✓

- 87.16 + 57.13 + 52.42 = 196.89
  196.89 - 52.42 - 57.31 = 87.16 ✓

Powers and Roots 1

Understanding Powers

Powers or indices show that a number is to be multiplied by itself a certain number of times.

4 x 4	$= 4^2$ (4 squared)
4 x 4 x 4	$= 4^3$ (4 cubed)
4 x 4 x 4 x 4	$= 4^4$ (4 to the power 4)

... and so on

$$4^2$$ ← the power or index

Square Numbers

Numbers obtained by squaring a number are called square numbers, for example...

4 squared $= 4^2 = 4 \times 4 = 16$

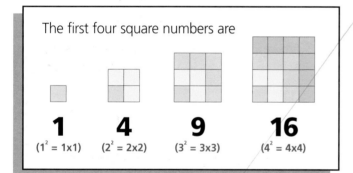

The first four square numbers are

1   4   9   16

$(1^2 = 1 \times 1)$ $(2^2 = 2 \times 2)$ $(3^2 = 3 \times 3)$ $(4^2 = 4 \times 4)$

Cube Numbers

Numbers obtained by cubing a number are called cube numbers, for example...

4 cubed $= 4^3 = 4 \times 4 \times 4 = 64$

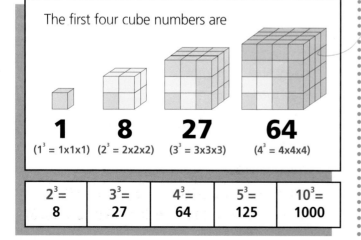

The first four cube numbers are

1   8   27   64

$(1^3 = 1 \times 1 \times 1)$ $(2^3 = 2 \times 2 \times 2)$ $(3^3 = 3 \times 3 \times 3)$ $(4^3 = 4 \times 4 \times 4)$

$2^3 =$	$3^3 =$	$4^3 =$	$5^3 =$	$10^3 =$
8	**27**	**64**	**125**	**1000**

Example...

Calculate the value of $2^2 \times 3^3$

$2^2 \times 3^3 = (2 \times 2) \times (3 \times 3 \times 3) = 4 \times 27 = 108$

Powers of 10

Large numbers can often be written more easily by using a power of 10. For instance **3×10^6** is another way of writing **3 000 000.**

$10^1 = 10$	(ten)
$10^2 = 100$	(one hundred)
$10^3 = 1000$	(one thousand)
$10^4 = 10\,000$	(ten thousand)
$10^5 = 100\,000$	(one hundred thousand)
$10^6 = 1\,000\,000$	(one million)

Powers of Negative Numbers

Great care is needed when working out powers of negative numbers. If you are in any doubt refer back to page 9 for the multiplication of integers.

Examples...

1 $(-4)^2 = -4 \times -4 = 16$

(since a 'minus' times a 'minus' is equal to a 'plus')

2 $(-4)^3 = -4 \times -4 \times -4 = -64$

(the first two 'minuses' give a 'plus'. This 'plus' times a 'minus' then gives a 'minus').

Rules of Indices

1 Powers are added when we multiply powers of the same number.

$3^5 \times 3^2 = 3^{5+2} = 3^7$, $10^3 \times 10 = 10^{3+1} = 10^4$

2 Powers are subtracted when we divide powers of the same number.

$3^5 \div 3^2 = 3^{5-2} = 3^3$, $10^3 \div 10 = 10^{3-1} = 10^2$

Also…

3 A number to a power of 1 is simply the number itself and vice versa.

$3^1 = 3$ and vice versa $3 = 3^1$

$10^1 = 10$ and vice versa $10 = 10^1$

4 A number to a power of 0 is always equal to 1.

$3^0 = 1$, $10^0 = 1$

Examples…

1 Evaluate $3^5 \times 3^7$

$= 3^{5+7}$

$= 3^{12}$

2 Evaluate $\dfrac{4^5}{4}$

$= 4^{5-1}$

$= 4^4$

3 Evaluate $\dfrac{3^4 \times 3^7}{3^8}$

$= \dfrac{3^{4+7}}{3^8}$ ← - Do the multiplication first.

$= 3^{11-8}$ ← - Then the division.

$= 3^3$

$= 27$

4 Evaluate $\dfrac{7^4 \times 7^5}{7 \times 7^8}$

$= \dfrac{7^{4+5}}{7^{1+8}}$

$= \dfrac{7^9}{7^9}$

$= 7^0$

$= 1$ ← Since any number to the power of 0 is equal to 1.

Square Roots

You know that…

$4^2 = 4 \times 4 = 16$

and also

$(-4)^2 = -4 \times -4 = 16$ (see previous page)

Another way of describing the above is to say that **+4 or -4 is the square root of 16**.

You can write 'the square root of 16' as $\sqrt{16}$ or $16^{\frac{1}{2}}$ ('16 to the power $\frac{1}{2}$') and so…

$\sqrt{16}$ or $16^{\frac{1}{2}} = \pm 4$ **(i.e. +4 or -4)**

This means that whenever you find the square root of a positive number there will always be a positive square root and a negative square root, for example…

$\sqrt{25}$ or $25^{\frac{1}{2}} = \pm 5$ **(i.e. +5 or -5)**

$\sqrt{36}$ or $36^{\frac{1}{2}} = \pm 6$ **(i.e. +6 or -6)**

You will be expected to be able to recall the square roots of all integer squares from 2^2 (4) to 15^2 (225)

$\sqrt{4}=$	$\sqrt{9}=$	$\sqrt{16}=$	$\sqrt{25}=$	$\sqrt{36}=$	$\sqrt{49}=$	$\sqrt{64}=$
±2	±3	±4	±5	±6	±7	±8

$\sqrt{81}=$	$\sqrt{100}=$	$\sqrt{121}=$	$\sqrt{144}=$	$\sqrt{169}=$	$\sqrt{196}=$	$\sqrt{225}=$
±9	±10	±11	±12	±13	±14	±15

Cube Roots

Finding the cube root of a positive number results in only one root… a positive root.

Since $4^3 = 4 \times 4 \times 4 = 64$,

then **4 is the cube root of 64**

You can write 'the cube root of 64' as $\sqrt[3]{64}$ or $64^{\frac{1}{3}}$ ('64 to the power $\frac{1}{3}$') and so…

$\sqrt[3]{64}$ or $64^{\frac{1}{3}} = 4$

Similarly…

$\sqrt[3]{125}$ or $125^{\frac{1}{3}} = 5$ (since $5 \times 5 \times 5 = 125$)

$\sqrt[3]{1000}$ or $1000^{\frac{1}{3}} = 10$ (since $10 \times 10 \times 10 = 1000$)

Standard Index Form

What is Standard Index Form?

If you are dealing with very large or very small numbers, it is not always practical to write them out in full each time. Standard Index Form, or Standard Form, is an alternative way of writing very large or very small numbers in shorthand.

To write a number in standard index form, you move its decimal point a certain number of places so that the number is written as $\mathbf{a \times 10^n}$… where $\mathbf{a}$ must be a number that is equal to or greater than **1** and less than **10**, and **n** is a positive or negative integer.

For **large** numbers greater than **1**, **n** is a **positive integer** and is equal to the number of places the decimal point has moved.

Examples…

1 $4372 = 4.372 \times 10^3$
$\rightarrow 4.372$
The decimal point has moved 3 places

2 $691000 = 6.91 \times 10^5$
$\rightarrow 6.91000$
The decimal point has moved 5 places

Numbers written in standard index form can also be converted to normal numbers…

3 $3.71 \times 10^4 = 37100$
$\rightarrow 37100.$

For **small** positive numbers less than **1**, **n** is a **negative integer** (**min**us for **min**ute numbers) and is equal to the number of places the decimal point has moved.

Examples…

1 $0.0356 = 3.56 \times 10^{-2}$
$\rightarrow 003.56$
The decimal point has moved 2 places

2 $0.00013 = 1.3 \times 10^{-4}$
$\rightarrow 00001.3$
The decimal point has moved 4 places

Numbers written in standard index form can also be written as normal numbers…

3 $4.5712 \times 10^{-5} = 0.000045712$
$\rightarrow .000045712$

Calculations with Standard Index Form

To ADD or SUBTRACT numbers written in standard index form, convert to 'normal numbers', do the calculation and then, if asked, change your answer back into standard index form.

To MULTIPLY or DIVIDE numbers written in standard index form, carry out separate calculations involving the numbers and powers and, if need be, rearrange your answer back into standard index form.

Examples…

1 $4.2 \times 10^4 + 8.6 \times 10^3$
$= 42000 + 8600$
$= 50600$
$= 5.06 \times 10^4$

2 $9.37 \times 10^{-2} - 1.6 \times 10^{-3}$
$= 0.0937 - 0.0016$
$= 0.0921$
$= 9.21 \times 10^{-2}$

Examples…

1 $3.2 \times 10^{-3} \times 4.5 \times 10^{-4}$
$= (3.2 \times 4.5) \times (10^{-3} \times 10^{-4})$
$= 14.4 \times 10^{-7}$
$= 1.44 \times 10^1 \times 10^{-7} = 1.44 \times 10^{-6}$

2 $5.6 \times 10^5 \div 8 \times 10^1$
$= (5.6 \div 8) \times (10^5 \div 10^1)$
$= 0.7 \times 10^4$
$= 7 \times 10^{-1} \times 10^4 = 7 \times 10^3$

Understanding Simple Fractions

The diagram shows a whole pizza that has been cut into four equal parts (or slices). Each slice can be described as a fraction of the whole pizza and its value is $\frac{1}{4}$.

The pizza however could have been cut into any number of slices, where each slice is a different fraction of the whole pizza (see the diagrams below).

The top number of a fraction is called the **numerator**, while the bottom number is called the **denominator**.

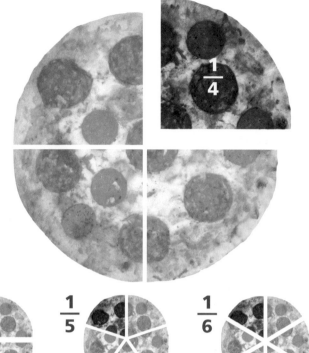

 $\frac{1}{2}$ 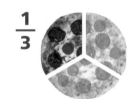 $\frac{1}{3}$ 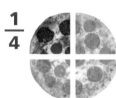 $\frac{1}{4}$ 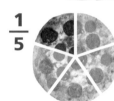 $\frac{1}{5}$  $\frac{1}{6}$

Equivalent Fractions

These are fractions that are equal. You can build chains of equivalent fractions by simply multiplying the numerator and denominator in the fraction by the same number.

① This chain was formed using the two times table.

$$\frac{1}{4} \; \overset{\times 2}{=} \; \frac{2}{8} \; \overset{\times 2}{=} \; \frac{4}{16} \; \overset{\times 2}{=} \; \frac{8}{32}$$

② This chain was formed using the three times table.

$$\frac{1}{5} \; \overset{\times 3}{=} \; \frac{3}{15} \; \overset{\times 3}{=} \; \frac{9}{45} \; \overset{\times 3}{=} \; \frac{27}{135}$$

Cancelling Fractions

You can also divide the numerator and denominator in a fraction by the same number to make them smaller. Chains of equivalent fractions that are cancelled down using division always come to an end when the fraction is expressed in its simplest form, i.e. lowest terms.

①
$$\frac{18}{27} \; \overset{\div 3}{=} \; \frac{6}{9} \; \overset{\div 3}{=} \; \frac{2}{3}$$

②
$$\frac{45}{60} \; \overset{\div 3}{=} \; \frac{15}{20} \; \overset{\div 5}{=} \; \frac{3}{4}$$

③
$$\frac{100}{140} \; \overset{\div 2}{=} \; \frac{50}{70} \; \overset{\div 2}{=} \; \frac{25}{35} \; \overset{\div 5}{=} \; \frac{5}{7}$$

Fractions 2

Ordering Fractions

To order fractions, write each fraction with a common denominator. If you are unsure choose the lowest common multiple of the denominators given. You can then order the fractions by the 'size' of the numerators, for example...

Arrange $\frac{9}{10}, \frac{4}{5}, \frac{7}{8}$ in ascending order.

Firstly write each fraction with a common denominator. The lowest common multiple of 10, 5 and 8 is 40.

Therefore...

$$\overset{\times 4}{\underset{\times 4}{\frac{9}{10}}} = \frac{36}{40} \qquad \overset{\times 8}{\underset{\times 8}{\frac{4}{5}}} = \frac{32}{40} \qquad \overset{\times 5}{\underset{\times 5}{\frac{7}{8}}} = \frac{35}{40}$$

If we now compare the numerators we can arrange the fractions in ascending (lowest to highest) order.

In ascending order they are: $\frac{4}{5}, \frac{7}{8}, \frac{9}{10}$

Also when you have fractions with common denominators it is possible to find other fractions that lie between these fractions.

For example, from above $\frac{4}{5} = \frac{32}{40}$ and $\frac{7}{8} = \frac{35}{40}$. It should be obvious that we can write two other fractions with denominator 40 which are greater than $\frac{4}{5}$ but less than $\frac{7}{8}$. They would be $\frac{33}{40}$ and $\frac{34}{40}$, which cancels down to $\frac{17}{20}$.

Improper Fractions and Mixed Numbers

Some fractions are known as improper because they are 'top heavy', i.e. the top number is bigger than the bottom number. $\frac{5}{4}$ is 'top heavy'. It needs simplifying into a mixed number so that it is easier to read and understand.

If we go back to our pizza on the previous page, then $\frac{5}{4}$ would be one whole pizza cut into four slices, plus one extra slice from another pizza.

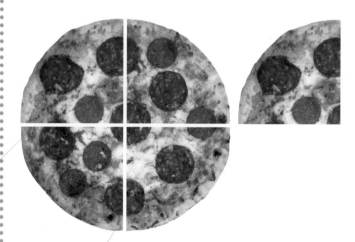

In other words...

$$\frac{5}{4} = \frac{4}{4} + \frac{1}{4} = 1\frac{1}{4}$$

Other Examples...

1 $\frac{13}{5} = \frac{5}{5} + \frac{5}{5} + \frac{3}{5} = 2\frac{3}{5}$

2 $\frac{19}{6} = \frac{6}{6} + \frac{6}{6} + \frac{6}{6} + \frac{1}{6} = 3\frac{1}{6}$

$19 \div 6 = 3 + \frac{1}{6}$ **left over!**

The examples above show improper fractions being changed into mixed numbers. The reverse process can also be used to change mixed numbers into improper fractions.

Addition of Fractions

Two fractions can be added very easily providing they have common denominators.

$$\frac{2}{5} = \frac{8}{20} \qquad \frac{2}{5} + \frac{3}{4} \qquad \frac{3}{4} = \frac{15}{20}$$
$$= \frac{8}{20} + \frac{15}{20}$$
$$= \frac{23}{20}$$
$$= 1\frac{3}{20}$$

With mixed numbers, add the whole numbers and fractions separately and then combine.

$$2\frac{2}{3} + 3\frac{1}{7}$$
$$= (2 + 3) + \left(\frac{2}{3} + \frac{1}{7}\right)$$
$$= \quad 5 \quad + \left(\frac{14}{21} + \frac{3}{21}\right)$$
$$= \quad 5 \quad + \quad \frac{17}{21} \quad = 5\frac{17}{21}$$

Subtraction of Fractions

As for addition, two fractions can be subtracted very easily providing they have common denominators.

$$\frac{7}{8} = \frac{21}{24} \qquad \frac{7}{8} - \frac{2}{3} \qquad \frac{2}{3} = \frac{16}{24}$$
$$= \frac{21}{24} - \frac{16}{24}$$
$$= \frac{5}{24}$$

With mixed numbers, subtract the whole numbers and fractions separately and then combine.

$$4\frac{1}{2} - 1\frac{4}{5}$$
$$= (4 - 1) + \left(\frac{1}{2} - \frac{4}{5}\right)$$
$$= \quad 3 \quad + \left(\frac{5}{10} - \frac{8}{10}\right)$$
$$= \quad 3 \quad + \left(-\frac{3}{10}\right)$$
$$= \quad 3 \quad - \quad \frac{3}{10}$$
$$= \left(2 + \frac{10}{10}\right) - \quad \frac{3}{10} = 2\frac{7}{10}$$

Multiplication and Division of Fractions

To multiply two fractions all you have to do is multiply together the two numerators and the two denominators.

$$\frac{2}{3} \times \frac{4}{5} = \frac{2 \times 4}{3 \times 5} = \frac{8}{15}$$

Division of two fractions is the same as multiplication, except that you turn the second fraction (that is doing the dividing) upside down and change the division sign to a multiplication sign.

$$\frac{2}{3} \div \frac{4}{5} = \frac{2}{3} \times \frac{5}{4} = \frac{2 \times 5}{3 \times 4} = \frac{10}{12} = \frac{5}{6}$$

To multiply or divide mixed numbers you have to change them to improper fractions first.

$$2\frac{1}{2} \times 1\frac{1}{6} = \frac{5}{2} \times \frac{7}{6} = \frac{5 \times 7}{2 \times 6} = \frac{35}{12} = 2\frac{11}{12}$$

$$1\frac{1}{3} \div 3\frac{1}{2} = \frac{4}{3} \div \frac{7}{2} = \frac{4}{3} \times \frac{2}{7} = \frac{4 \times 2}{3 \times 7} = \frac{8}{21}$$

To multiply or divide a fraction by an integer, change the integer to an improper fraction. For example, **4** as an improper fraction is $\frac{4}{1}$. You can then do the multiplication or division as normal.

$$\frac{4}{7} \times 3 = \frac{4}{7} \times \frac{3}{1} = \frac{4 \times 3}{7 \times 1} = \frac{12}{7} = 1\frac{5}{7}$$

$$\frac{2}{3} \div 10 = \frac{2}{3} \div \frac{10}{1} = \frac{2}{3} \times \frac{1}{10} = \frac{2 \times 1}{3 \times 10} = \frac{2}{30} = \frac{1}{15}$$

Calculations Involving Fractions

Calculating a Fraction of a Quantity

To find a fraction of any quantity all you have to do is multiply the fraction by the quantity. In other words, 'of' means 'times' or 'multiply' (x).

£9,000

Examples...

1 Calculate $\frac{4}{5}$ of 60kg.

'of' means 'x'

$\frac{4}{5}$ of 60kg = $\frac{4}{5}$ x 60

$= \frac{4}{5} \times \frac{60}{1}$

$= \frac{240}{5}$

$= 48kg$

2 A brand new car costing £9000 will lose $\frac{1}{5}$ of its value in the first year. What is the value of the car after the first year?

Before we can calculate its value we need to calculate the loss.

'of' means 'x'

Loss = $\frac{1}{5}$ of £9000 = $\frac{1}{5}$ x 9000 = $\frac{1}{5}$ x $\frac{9000}{1}$ = $\frac{9000}{5}$ = £1800

Value of car after the first year = £9000 - £1800 = £7200.

Expressing One Quantity as a Fraction of Another Quantity

Firstly, you must make sure that both quantities are in the same units. Then, to express the relationship as a fraction, the first quantity becomes the numerator (top number) and the second quantity becomes the denominator (bottom number). If need be, write the fraction in its lowest terms.

Examples...

1 Write 30 out of 120 as a fraction.

30 out of 120 = $\frac{30}{120}$ = $\frac{1}{4}$

2 Express 36 seconds as a fraction of 2 minutes. Both quantities must be in the same units, so change 2 minutes into seconds.

2 minutes = 2 x 60s = 120s, so...

36s as a fraction of 120s = $\frac{36}{120}$ = $\frac{3}{10}$

Understanding Simple Decimals

When you use money and metric measures, such as millimetres, litres or grams, you often use simple decimals. Decimals are an easy kind of fraction - easy because the ten 'times' table is the only one ever needed! If you think of a pizza, with decimals the whole pizza is only ever divided into ten, a hundred or a thousand pieces.

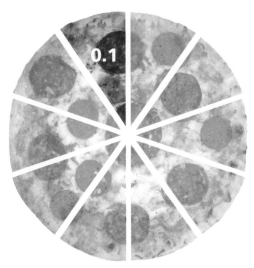

where each slice = $\frac{1}{10}$ or **0.1**

 0.1    0.2   0.3   0.4   0.5   etc.

Place Value in Decimal Numbers

We have already seen that all the digits in a whole number have a place value. In a decimal number, all digits to the right of the decimal point also have a place value.

Decimal Number	Place Value of Digits					
	10	1	**•**	$\frac{1}{10}$	$\frac{1}{100}$	$\frac{1}{1000}$
	Tens	Units	DECIMAL POINT	Tenths	Hundredths	Thousandths
0.06		0		0	6	
0.507		0		5	0	7
1.39		1		3	9	
74.258	7	4		2	5	8

The position of the decimal point is just as important as the digits themselves. Misplacing the decimal point makes a huge difference because all the place values change. For example, in a long jump contest a pupil records a jump of 4.37m. Imagine the excitement if the distance was recorded as 43.7m!

Decimals and Money

An amount of money is often written as a decimal, where the decimal point separates the amount in pounds from the amount in pence. Remember, any amount of money involving pounds and pence is always written to 2 decimal places (2d.p.), for example…

- Six pounds forty seven pence is written as **£6.47**

- Twelve pounds one pence is written as **£12.01 and not £12.1**

- £5 can be written as **£5.00**

- 47p can be written as **£0.47**

Decimals 2

Recurring and Terminating Decimals

$\frac{1}{3}$ as a decimal is 0.33333333... and so on

$\frac{3}{11}$ as a decimal is 0.27272727... and so on

Both of these are examples of recurring decimals because one or more of the digits repeats itself continuously. To make it simpler we place a dot (•) over the digit or digits that repeat continuously.

$\frac{1}{3}$ = 0.33333333... = 0.$\dot{3}$

$\frac{3}{11}$ = 0.27272727... = 0.$\dot{2}\dot{7}$

Decimals that do not recur are called terminating decimals. Fractions, written in their **simplest form**, will convert into terminating decimals **if** their denominators have prime factors of either **2** or **5** or **both**.

$\frac{7}{10}$ = **0.7** (since 10 = 2 x 5)

$\frac{5}{8}$ = **0.625** (since 8 = 2 x 2 x 2)

$\frac{19}{50}$ = **0.38** (since 50 = 2 x 5 x 5)

Ordering Decimals

This means rearranging a series of decimals in either ascending (lowest to highest) or descending (highest to lowest) order. A useful method is to line up all the decimal points of the numbers in a vertical line. Then you can start with the first column on the left, and work along each column of numbers (left to right) to decide which is the biggest number.

Example...

Rearrange the following in ascending order:
0.54, 5.4, 0.45, 4.5

Line up the decimal points.

0.54	0.45
5.4	0.54
0.45	4.5
4.5	5.4

Addition and Subtraction of Decimals

As for whole numbers the place values of the digits must line up one on top of the other, although an easy way is to simply line up your decimal points. Do remember to bring the decimal point down to your answer.

Examples...

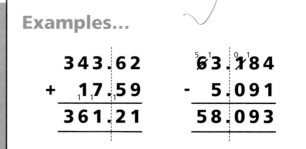

$$343.62 + 17.59 = 361.21$$

$$63.184 - 5.091 = 58.093$$

Multiplication with Decimals

Multiplication of Decimal Numbers by Powers of 10

To multiply a decimal number by a power of 10 e.g. 10 (10^1), 100 (10^2), 1000 (10^3), all you have to do is move all the digits a certain number of place values to the left. When you do this your number becomes bigger. For example…

① 9.32 x 10 = 93.2

Digits move one place value to the left and the number becomes 10 times bigger.

② 0.047 x 100 = 4.7

Digits move two place values to the left and the number becomes 100 times bigger.

③ 13.27 x 1000 = 13 270

Digits move three place values to the left and the number becomes 1000 times bigger.

Multiplication of Positive Numbers by Decimal Numbers between 0 and 1

If you multiply any positive number by a decimal number between 0 and 1 the answer is always smaller than the positive number you started with, for example…

① 10 x 0.5 = 5

② 5 x 0.3 = 1.5

③ 986 x 0.01 = 9.86

Multiplication of Decimal Numbers by Whole and Decimal Numbers

All you do is ignore the decimal points and multiply as you would whole numbers. You put the decimal point in at the end. In your answer, the number of digits after the decimal point should be the same as the total number of digits after the decimal points in the numbers being multiplied. For example…

① 2.73 x 18

Multiply as you would whole numbers (see page 7)

```
      273
   x   18
    ─────
     2730
     2184
    ─────
     4914
```

Then, count the digits after the decimal point in the numbers being multiplied and transfer to answer.

2.73 x 18 = 49.14

Therefore **2.73 x 18 = 49.14**

② 17.5 x 9.61

Multiply as you would whole numbers.

```
       175
    x  961
   ───────
   157500
    10500
      175
   ───────
   168175
```

Then, count the digits after the decimal point in the numbers being multiplied and transfer to answer.

17.5 x 9.61 = 168.175

Therefore **17.5 x 9.61 = 168.175**

Division with Decimals

Division of Decimal Numbers by Powers of 10

The process is the reverse of multiplying decimal numbers by powers of 10. With division all the digits move a certain number of place values to the right. When you do this your number becomes smaller. For example…

1 $46.3 \div 10 = 4.63$

Digits move one place value to the right and the number becomes 10 times smaller.

2 $3.615 \div 100 = 0.03615$

Digits move two place values to the right and the number becomes 100 times smaller.

3 $473.2 \div 1000 = 0.4732$

Digits move three place values to the right and the number becomes 1000 times smaller.

Division of Positive Numbers by Decimal Numbers between 0 and 1

If you divide any positive number by a decimal number between 0 and 1 the answer is always bigger than the positive number you started with, for example…

1 $10 \div 0.5 = 20$

2 $5 \div 0.4 = 12.5$

3 $471 \div 0.01 = 47\ 100$

Division of Decimal Numbers by Whole and Decimal Numbers

Division of a decimal number by a whole number is the same as the division of whole numbers (see page 7). The only exception is that you must remember to take the decimal point up to your answer.

$13.2 \div 6$
Divide as you would whole numbers

$$
\begin{array}{r}
2.2 \\
6\overline{)13.2} \\
12 \\
\hline
1\ 2 \\
1\ 2 \\
\hline
0
\end{array}
$$

Remember to take the decimal point up to the answer

Therefore **$13.2 \div 6 = 2.2$**

Division of a decimal number by another decimal number is slightly more tricky. Before you start, multiply both numbers by 10, 100, etc. until the number doing the dividing is a whole number. The process from now on is the same as the example above.

$4.368 \div 0.56$
Multiply both numbers by 100 to make the number doing the dividing a whole number.
$4.368 \times 100 = 436.8$, $0.56 \times 100 = 56$
Divide as you would whole numbers.

$$
\begin{array}{r}
7.8 \\
56\overline{)436.8} \\
392 \\
\hline
44\ 8 \\
44\ 8 \\
\hline
0
\end{array}
$$

Remember to take the decimal point up to the answer

Therefore **$4.368 \div 0.56 = 7.8$**

Understanding Simple Percentages

Percentages are used in everyday life, from pay rises to price reductions. This helps us to make easy comparisons. When you understand the basics of percentages they are even easier than decimals or fractions. They focus on the whole being equal to one hundred, i.e. the whole is one hundred per cent. So, if someone gives you 50% of a whole pizza this tells you the 'number of parts per 100' you have, e.g. 50% is 50 parts per 100 or $\frac{50}{100}$

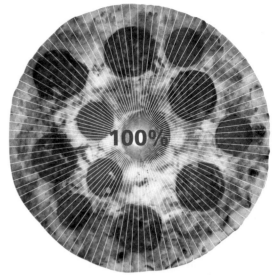

100%

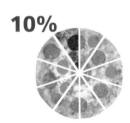  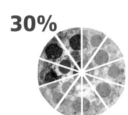 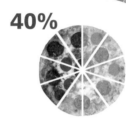 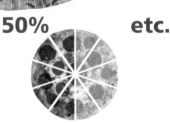

10%   **20%**   **30%**   **40%**   **50%**   **etc.**

Calculating a Percentage of a Quantity

Examples...

1 Calculate 40% of 50cm.

40% means 40 parts per 100 or $\frac{40}{100}$ and 'of' means 'times' or 'multiply'(x).

$$40\% \text{ of } 50cm = \frac{40}{100} \times 50 = \frac{40 \times 50}{100}$$

$$= 20cm$$

2 Calculate 15% of £4.80. Give your answer in pence.

£4.80 = 4.80 x 100p = 480p

15% means 15 parts out of 100 or $\frac{15}{100}$ and 'of' means 'times' (x).

$$15\% \text{ of } 480p = \frac{15}{100} \times 480$$

$$= \frac{15 \times 480}{100}$$

$$= 72p$$

Expressing One Quantity as a Percentage of Another Quantity

Make sure that both quantities are in the same units. Firstly, express one quantity as a fraction of the other, where the first quantity becomes the numerator (top number) and the second quantity becomes the denominator (bottom number). Then all you have to do is multiply this fraction by 100%.

Examples...

1 Write 18 out of 30 as a percentage.

$$18 \text{ out of } 30 = \frac{18}{30} \times 100\%$$

$$= \frac{18 \times 100}{30} = 60\%$$

2 Express 30cm as a percentage of 3m. Both quantities must be in the same units, so change 3m into centimetres.

3m = 3 x 100cm = 300cm, so...

$$30cm \text{ as a } \% \text{ of } 300cm = \frac{30}{300} \times 100\%$$

$$= \frac{30 \times 100}{300} = 10\%$$

Percentages 2

Examples...

1 A standard box of breakfast cereal weighs 500g. Special boxes contain an extra 25%. Calculate the weight of a special box of cereal.

> Firstly calculate the extra increase in weight...

$$25\% \text{ of } 500g = \frac{25}{100} \times 500g$$
$$= \frac{25 \times 500}{100} = 125g$$

> ... then add it to the weight of a standard box of cereal.

Weight of special box = 500g + 125g
= 625g

An alternative method would be as follows: A standard box of cereal is to be increased by 25%. If a standard box is 100%, a special box will be 100% + 25% = 125%.

$$125\% = \frac{125}{100} = 1.25$$

> In other words, the weight of a special box is 1.25 times the weight of a standard box.

Weight of special box = 1.25 x 500g
= 625g

2 On 1st January 2002 John buys a house for £100 000. If house price inflation then runs at 15% per annum for the next two years, how much will his house be worth...
a) on December 31st 2002?
b) on December 31st 2003?

a) **Original cost = £100 000**

$$£100\,000 \times \frac{115}{100}$$

> $\frac{115}{100}$ represents a 15% increase

= £115 000

b) **Cost after 1 year = £115 000**

$$£115\,000 \times \frac{115}{100}$$

> $\frac{115}{100}$ represents a 15% increase

= £132 250

3 On 1st January John's weight is 80kg. In the first six months of the year his weight increases by 10%, followed by a 10% decrease in the second six months of the year. What is his weight at the end of the year?

After the first six months, his weight is **100% + 10% = 110%** of his original weight.
$$110\% = \frac{110}{100} = 1.1$$

> i.e. his weight is now 1.1 times its original amount.

After the second six months, his weight is **100% - 10% = 90%** of his weight at the end of the first six months.

$$90\% = \frac{90}{100} = 0.9$$

> i.e. his weight becomes 0.9 times the previous amount, which is actually a decrease.

Weight at end of year
= 1.1 x 0.9 x 80kg = 79.2kg

4 A bouncing ball is dropped from a height of 5m. It reaches 80% of its previous height after every bounce. How high does it reach after the third bounce?

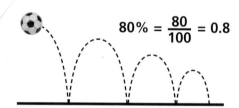

$$80\% = \frac{80}{100} = 0.8$$

> So, the height the ball reaches is 0.8 times the previous height reached.

After 3 bounces, height reached
= 0.8 x 0.8 x 0.8 x 5m = 2.56m

Alternatively, this is an example of a repeated multiplier. In other words $0.8 \times 0.8 \times 0.8 = 0.8^3$ (0.8 to the power 3) to give us...

After 3 bounces, height reached
= 0.8^3 x 5m = 0.512 x 5m = 2.56m

Calculations Involving Comparisons

These are calculations where the original amount has been increased or decreased by a certain percentage to a transformed amount. You must remember that the original amount is always equal to 100% and that the transformed amount will always be a percentage that is above or below 100%.

Examples...

1 A shop offers 10% off all its clothes. A shirt has a sale price of £27. What was the original price of the shirt?

Original price of shirt = 100%
Sale price of shirt = 100% - 10%

| There has been a decrease of 10% | **= 90%** |

$$\therefore \quad \begin{array}{c} \div 90 \\ \times 100 \end{array} \left\{ \begin{array}{l} \textbf{90\% = £27} \\ \textbf{1\% = £0.30} \\ \textbf{100\% = £30} \end{array} \right\} \begin{array}{c} \div 90 \\ \times 100 \end{array}$$

So the original price of the shirt was £30

2 In 2006 a company allocated £15 000 of its budget to be spent on advertising. This was a 20% increase on the money spent on advertising in 2005. How much money did the company spend on advertising in 2005?

| Original amount in this question is the money spent on advertising in 2005. |

2005

Money spent on advertising in 2005 = 100%
Money spent on advertising in 2006 = 100% + 20%

| There has been an increase of 20% | **= 120%** |

$$\therefore \quad \begin{array}{c} \div 120 \\ \times 100 \end{array} \left\{ \begin{array}{l} \textbf{120\% = £15 000} \\ \textbf{1\% = £125} \\ \textbf{100\% = £12 500} \end{array} \right\} \begin{array}{c} \div 120 \\ \times 100 \end{array}$$

So the advertising budget for 2005 was £12 500

2006

Converting Between Systems

Below is a summary of how to convert between fractions, decimals and percentages. You may start at any of the three points. Trace around the charts and see how you can move from one system to another by following simple rules.

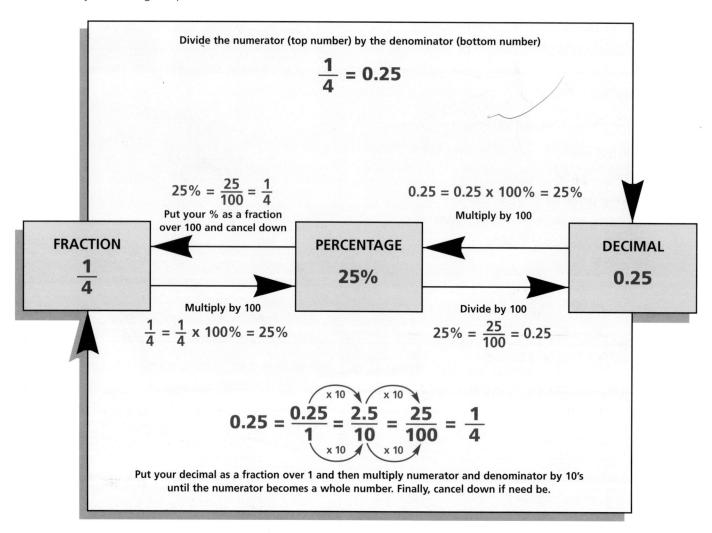

Divide the numerator (top number) by the denominator (bottom number)

$$\frac{1}{4} = 0.25$$

$25\% = \frac{25}{100} = \frac{1}{4}$
Put your % as a fraction over 100 and cancel down

$0.25 = 0.25 \times 100\% = 25\%$
Multiply by 100

FRACTION $\frac{1}{4}$	**PERCENTAGE** 25%	**DECIMAL** 0.25

Multiply by 100
$\frac{1}{4} = \frac{1}{4} \times 100\% = 25\%$

Divide by 100
$25\% = \frac{25}{100} = 0.25$

$$0.25 = \frac{0.25}{1} = \frac{2.5}{10} = \frac{25}{100} = \frac{1}{4}$$
(x 10, x 10)

Put your decimal as a fraction over 1 and then multiply numerator and denominator by 10's until the numerator becomes a whole number. Finally, cancel down if need be.

Other Examples...

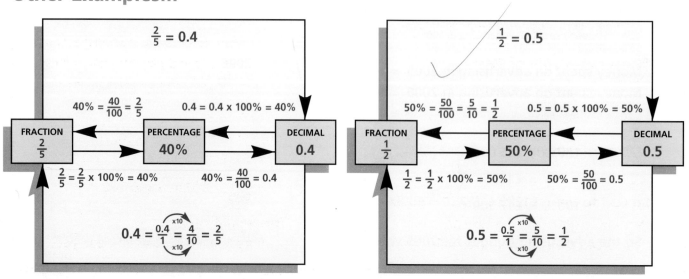

$$\frac{2}{5} = 0.4$$

$40\% = \frac{40}{100} = \frac{2}{5}$ $0.4 = 0.4 \times 100\% = 40\%$

FRACTION $\frac{2}{5}$	**PERCENTAGE** 40%	**DECIMAL** 0.4

$\frac{2}{5} = \frac{2}{5} \times 100\% = 40\%$ $40\% = \frac{40}{100} = 0.4$

$$0.4 = \frac{0.4}{1} = \frac{4}{10} = \frac{2}{5}$$

$$\frac{1}{2} = 0.5$$

$50\% = \frac{50}{100} = \frac{5}{10} = \frac{1}{2}$ $0.5 = 0.5 \times 100\% = 50\%$

FRACTION $\frac{1}{2}$	**PERCENTAGE** 50%	**DECIMAL** 0.5

$\frac{1}{2} = \frac{1}{2} \times 100\% = 50\%$ $50\% = \frac{50}{100} = 0.5$

$$0.5 = \frac{0.5}{1} = \frac{5}{10} = \frac{1}{2}$$

VAT

Value Added Tax or VAT is charged on goods you buy or any services you receive. Penny wants to buy this radio cassette player. How much will it cost her if VAT is charged at a rate of $17\frac{1}{2}$%?

$$VAT = 17\frac{1}{2}\% \text{ of } £50$$

$$= \frac{17\frac{1}{2}}{100} \times £50$$

$$= £8.75$$

Therefore total cost

$$= £50 + £8.75$$

$$= £58.75$$

Purchasing on Credit

This is when you pay a deposit on a purchase and then you make a number of repayments spread over a certain period of time.

Example...

Jim is buying a car on credit. How much will it cost him altogether?

£6,000
or 20% Deposit
& 36 monthly
repayments of £160

20% deposit = 20% of £6000

$$= \frac{20}{100} \times 6000$$

$$= £1200$$

Total cost of repayments = 36 × £160

$$= £5760$$

Total cost to Jim = £1200 + £5760 = £6960

(This is £960 more than the cash price but he has spread the cost over 36 months)

Simple Interest

1 Mr and Mrs Smith have just won £10 000 on the lottery. They decide that they want to invest this money for 2 years. Mr Smith wants to invest the money at 6% simple interest. How much interest will he gain after 2 years?

Interest gained after 1st year

= 6% of £10 000

$$= \frac{6}{100} \times £10\ 000 = £600$$

> With simple interest the interest gained (£600) is not added to the amount invested so it does not earn interest in the next year

Interest gained after 2nd year

= £600 (same as 1st year)

Total interest gained

= £600 + £600 = £1200

2 If they put the money in a special account for 5 years it would pay terminal interest of 33%. Would this be better than 6% per year for 5 years?

Interest gained after 5 years

= 33% of £10 000

$$= \frac{33}{100} \times £10\ 000 = £3300$$

This would compare to

5 × £600 = £3000 at 6% per year

Everyday Maths 2

Household Bills

More times than not these are worked out using 'common sense'. Here is a home-owner's electricity bill for one quarter:

The number of units used is found by subtracting the two meter readings

Meter Reading

	Present	Previous	Units used	Pence per unit	Amount
	25081	24295	786	7.5	58.95
				Quarterly charge	10.45
				Total charged this quarter excluding VAT	69.40
				VAT at 5%	3.47
				Total payable	£72.87

786 units x 7.5 pence per unit = £58.95

You have to pay this regardless of how much electricity you use

5% of £69.40
= $\frac{5}{100}$ x £69.40
= £3.47

£69.40 + £3.47 = £72.87

Understanding Tables and Charts

The secret to understanding tables and charts is to identify the relevant data. Once you've done this all you need to use is a bit of 'common sense'.

Example...

A rail company operating trains out of Petersfield decides to offer cheap 'Off Peak' fares on services that arrive at London Waterloo after 10am. If a customer who usually catches the 0833 service from Petersfield decides to wait for the first Off Peak train, to take advantage of the offer, what will be the difference in his journey time?

The first thing to do is to identify the relevant data. This is in the third and fourth columns of the timetable shown opposite and has been highlighted for this purpose.

Usual journey time = Arrival Time - Departure Time

Remember to calculate hours & minutes separately

= 0939hrs - 0833hrs

= 1hr 6min

Off Peak journey time = Arrival Time - Departure Time

= 1018hrs - 0901hrs

= 1hr 17min

Difference in time = 1hr 17min - 1hr 6min

= 11min

Petersfield, Millford, Farncombe, Woking to London Waterloo

Mondays to Fridays

	AN	NW	AN	AN	AN
Petersfield	0752	0811	0833	0901	0928
Liphook	——	——	——	——	——
Haslemere	——	——	——	——	——
Witley	——	——	——	——	——
Millford (Surrey)	0806	0829	0845	0917	0941
Godalming	——	——	——	——	——
Farncombe	0822	0850	0900	0937	0959
Guildford	——	——	——	——	——
Reading	——	——	——	——	——
Woking	0830	0900	0907	0947	1007
Heathrow Airport (T1)	——	——	——	——	——
Clapham Junction	——	——	——	——	——
London Waterloo	0903	0932	0939	1018	1036

Mondays to Fridays

	AN	NW	AN	AN	AN
Petersfield	0949	0956	1019	1049	1055
Liphook	——	——	——	——	——
Haslemere	——	——	——	——	——
Witley	——	——	——	——	——
Millford (Surrey)	1002	1011	1032	1102	1114
Godalming	——	——	——	——	——
Farncombe	1017	1032	1047	1117	1132
Guildford	——	——	——	——	——
Reading	——	——	——	——	——
Woking	1026	1043	1059	1128	1142
Heathrow Airport (T1)	——	——	——	——	——
Clapham Junction	——	——	——	——	——
London Waterloo	1052	1111	1125	1155	1211

Ratio and Proportion 1

What is a Ratio?

A ratio is a comparison between two or more quantities. Here we have two columns of coins. The first column has ten £1 coins and the second column has six 2p coins. To compare the two sets of coins we can say that the ratio of the number of £1 coins to 2p coins is **10 to 6 or 10 : 6**

This is like saying $\frac{10}{16}$ are £1 coins while $\frac{6}{16}$ are 2p coins. Ratios can be simplified into their simplest form, just like fractions…

$$\div2 \left(\begin{array}{c} \mathbf{10 : 6} \\ \mathbf{= 5 : 3} \end{array} \right) \div2$$

A ratio of **5 : 3** means that for every five £1 coins there are three 2p coins. The above ratio can also be written in the form **1 : n** by dividing both numbers in the ratio by 5…

$$\div5 \left(\begin{array}{c} \mathbf{5 : 3} \\ \mathbf{= 1 : 0.6} \end{array} \right) \div5$$

It could be written in the form **n : 1** by dividing both numbers in the ratio by 3…

$$\div3 \left(\begin{array}{c} \mathbf{5 : 3} \\ \mathbf{= 1.\dot{6} : 1} \end{array} \right) \div3$$

Example

A bag of carrots weighs 300g and a bag of potatoes 1.5kg. Calculate the ratio of weight of carrots to weight of potatoes.

Both quantities must be in the same units so, **1.5kg = 1.5 x 1000g = 1 500g**

Ratio of weight of carrots to weight of potatoes is…

$$\div300 \left(\begin{array}{c} \mathbf{300g : 1500g} \\ \mathbf{= 1 : 5} \end{array} \right) \div300$$

Ratios and Fractions

A ratio can be written as a fraction and vice versa.

Example

If $\frac{2}{5}$ of a class are boys what is the ratio of boys to girls? Give your answer in the form 1 : n.

The ratio of boys to girls is therefore…

$$\times5 \left(\begin{array}{c} \frac{2}{5} : \frac{3}{5} \\ \mathbf{= 2 : 3} \end{array} \right) \times5$$

Written in the form **1 : n** it is…

$$\div2 \left(\begin{array}{c} \mathbf{2 : 3} \\ \mathbf{= 1 : 1.5} \end{array} \right) \div2$$

In other words for any one boy in the class there are one and a half girls!

Ratio and Proportion 2

Dividing a Quantity in a Given Ratio

Examples...

①

£60 is to be divided between Jon and Pat in the ratio 2 : 3. How much money does each one receive?

> We need to divide £60 in the ratio 2 : 3

The digits in the ratio represent parts. Jon gets 2 parts and Pat gets 3 parts. The total number of parts is **2 + 3 = 5 parts** which is equal to £60. Therefore...

$$\div5 \left(\begin{array}{l} \textbf{5 parts } = \textbf{£60} \\ \textbf{1 part } = \textbf{£12} \end{array} \right) \div5$$

Since we now know the 'value' of 1 part we can work out how much money Jon and Pat get.

Jon gets 2 parts = 2 x £12 = £24
Pat gets 3 parts = 3 x £12 = £36

> Check: £24 + £36 = £60

② Three brothers aged 6, 9 and 15 decide grudgingly to share a tin of toffees in the ratio of their ages. If the tin contains 240 toffees how many toffees does each brother get?

> We need to divide 240 toffees in the ratio 6 : 9 : 15

> Whenever possible cancel down your ratio to make things simpler

$$\div3 \left(\begin{array}{l} \textbf{6 : 9 : 15} \\ \textbf{= 2 : 3 : 5} \end{array} \right) \div3$$

Total number of parts
= 2 + 3 + 5 = 10 parts

Therefore...

$$\div10 \left(\begin{array}{l} \textbf{10 parts = 240 toffees} \\ \textbf{1 part = 24 toffees} \end{array} \right) \div10$$

Brother aged 6 gets 2 x 24 = 48 toffees
Brother aged 9 gets 3 x 24 = 72 toffees
Brother aged 15 gets 5 x 24 = 120 toffees

> Check: 48 + 72 + 120 = 240 toffees

Increasing and Decreasing a Quantity in Direct Proportion

Example...

A recipe to make 10 flapjack cakes requires, among other ingredients, 180g of butter. How much butter does a cook need to use if she wants to make
a) 6 flapjack cakes?
b) 25 flapjack cakes?

This is an example of a quantity (e.g. butter) that increases or decreases in direct proportion to the amount of cakes needed. The more cakes that are needed the greater the amount of butter needed and vice versa.

> The easiest way is to work out the amount of butter needed to make 1 flapjack cake.

$$\div10 \left(\begin{array}{l} \textbf{10 cakes require 180g of butter} \\ \textbf{1 cake requires 18g of butter} \end{array} \right) \div10$$

a) 6 flapjack cakes require
6 x 18g = 108g of butter

b) 25 flapjack cakes require
25 x 18g = 450g of butter

The Basics of Algebra 1

Algebra is a branch of mathematics where letters and other symbols are used to represent numbers and quantities in expressions, equations, identities and formulae. Algebra follows the same rules as arithmetic.

Algebraic Expressions

An algebraic expression is a collection of connected letters, numbers and arithmetical symbols. Here are some simple expressions and their meanings.

Algebraic Expression	What it means
2a	a + a or 2 x a
ab	a x b (or b x a)
$\frac{a}{b}$	a ÷ b
3a - b	(3 x a) - b
c^2	c x c
4mn	4 x m x n
x^2	x x x
a^3	a x a x a
$4x^2y$	4 x x x x x y
$(4a)^2$	4a x 4a

Collecting Like Terms

Many expressions can be simplified by collecting together like terms.

Examples...

1 **a + 2a** is more simply **3a**

2 **5x - 8x + 7x** is more simply **4x**

When your expression contains 'different' like terms, rearrange and collect together all like terms before you simplify.

3   **6b + 3c - 4b**

= <u>6b - 4b</u> + 3c
   Like terms

= **2b + 3c**

4   **- 4x + 3 + 7x - 8**

= <u>- 4x + 7x</u> + <u>3 - 8</u>
  Like terms   Like terms

= **3x - 5**

5   **4x + 7y - x - 3y**

= <u>4x - x</u> + <u>7y - 3y</u>
  Like terms   Like terms

= **3x + 4y**

6   **5pq - 7rs + 8qp + 2sr**

= <u>5pq + 8pq</u> - <u>7rs + 2rs</u>

  Like terms   Like terms
  since 'pq' is the since 'rs' is the
  same as 'qp'   same as 'sr'

= **13pq - 5rs.**

Identities

a + a + a = 3a and **a + 2a = 3a** are both examples of identities and not equations, because **a + a + a** and **a + 2a** are simply different ways of expressing **3a**. What we have on the left-hand side of the equal sign is no different to what we have on the right-hand side. This means that **a** could take any value and they would both hold true. **5x - 8x + 7x = 4x** is another example of an identity.

The Basics of Algebra 2

Rules of Indices for Algebra

The same rules are used with letters as we previously used with numbers (see page 15). Very simply…

1 $x^5 \times x^2$ becomes x^{5+2} and is equal to x^7
… we add the powers.

2 $x^5 \div x^2$ becomes x^{5-2} and is equal to x^3
… we subtract the powers.

Also…

3 x^1 is the same as x… and vice versa
… x is the same as x^1.

4 x^0 is equal to 1 … anything to the power of 0 (zero) is always equal to 1.

5 x^{-1} is the same as $\frac{1}{x}$ … and vice versa
… $\frac{1}{x}$ is the same as x^{-1}.

Examples…

1 $2x^3 \times 4x^2$

$= (2 \times 4)\, x^{3+2}$

$= 8x^5$

> Multiply your numbers as normal and add the powers

2 $10r^5 \div 2r$

$= \left(\dfrac{10}{2}\right) r^{5-1}$

$= 5r^4$

> Divide your numbers as normal and subtract the powers

3 $\dfrac{5r^3 \times 4r^2}{10r^6}$

$= \dfrac{(5 \times 4)r^{3+2}}{10r^6}$

> Do one operation at a time. Multiplication first…

$= \left(\dfrac{20}{10}\right) r^{5-6}$

> … and then division

$= 2r^{-1} \left(= \dfrac{2}{r}\right)$

4 $x^4y^2 \times x^3y^6$

$= x^{4+3}\, y^{2+6}$

$= x^7y^8$

> Add the powers of x's and y's separately

5 $12p^5r^4 \div 6p^5r^3$

$= \left(\dfrac{12}{6}\right) p^{5-5}r^{4-3}$

> Divide your numbers as normal. Subtract the powers of p's and r's separately

$= 2r$

> Remember $p^0 = 1$

Lonsdale

This involves substituting numbers for letters in expressions. The simplest substitution would involve only one operation (e.g. an addition or multiplication). However, when a substitution involves more than one operation, you must make them in the order shown below.

Also, since you are expected to be able to substitute positive and negative numbers into expressions turn back to page 9 to refresh yourself on the multiplication and division of integers.

BIDMAS

BRACKETS   INDICES   DIVISIONS AND MULTIPLICATIONS - THESE CAN BE DONE IN ANY ORDER   ADDITIONS AND SUBTRACTIONS - AGAIN IN ANY ORDER

Examples...

If **a = 3, b = 8, c = 20, d = -4,** calculate the value of…

1 $2(a + b) - c$ Substitute in your numbers

$= 2(3 + 8) - 20$ Work out the bracket first

$= 2 \times 11 - 20$ Then the multiplication

$= 22 - 20$ Then the subtraction

$= 2$

2 $\dfrac{c(d + 1)}{5}$ Substitute in your numbers

$= \dfrac{20(-4 +1)}{5}$ Work out the bracket first

$= \dfrac{20 \times -3}{5}$ Then the multiplication (+ x - = -)

$= \dfrac{-60}{5}$ Then the division (- ÷ + = -)

$= -12$

3 $3d^2 + c$ Substitute in your numbers

$= 3 \times (-4)^2 + 20$ Work out the square first (- x - = +)

$= 3 \times 16 + 20$ Then the multiplication

$= 48 + 20$ Then the addition

$= 68$

4 $2a^3$ Substitute in your numbers

$= 2 \times (3)^3$ Work out the cube first

$= 2 \times 27$ Then the multiplication

$= 54$

5 $\dfrac{1}{2}d^3$ Substitute in your numbers

$= \dfrac{1}{2} \times (-4)^3$ Work out the cube first (- x - = + and then + x - = -)

$= \dfrac{1}{2} \times -64$ Then the multiplication

$= -32$

Brackets and Factorisation

Multiplying Out Brackets

When we multiply out a bracket, everything which is inside the bracket must be multiplied by whatever is immediately outside the bracket.

Examples...

1 $4(x+3)$

$= 4 \times x + 4 \times 3$

$= 4x + 12$

2 $6(3x + 2)$

$= 6 \times 3x + 6 \times 2$

$= 18x + 12$

3 $4(5x - 4)$

$= 4 \times 5x + 4 \times -4$

$= 20x - 16$

4 $5(2x + 7)$

$= 5 \times 2x + 5 \times 7$

$= 10x + 35$

5 $x(x + 3) - 7$

$= x \times x + x \times 3 - 7$

$= x^2 + 3x - 7$

If your expression includes two brackets you may end up with like terms, which you need to collect together and simplify.

6 $2(4x + 3) + 5(x - 2)$

$= 2 \times 4x + 2 \times 3 + 5 \times x + 5 \times -2$

$= 8x + 6 + 5x - 10$

$= \underbrace{8x + 5x}_{\text{Like terms}} + \underbrace{6 - 10}_{\text{Like terms}}$

$= 13x - 4$

7 $x(5 - x) + 4x(2x^2 + 3x)$

$= x \times 5 + x \times -x + 4x \times 2x^2 + 4x \times 3x$

$= 5x - x^2 + 8x^3 + 12x^2$

$= 8x^3 \underbrace{- x^2 + 12x^2}_{\text{Like terms}} + 5x$

$= 8x^3 + 11x^2 + 5x$

When you multiply out two brackets make sure that each term in the second bracket is multiplied by each term in the first bracket.

8 $(x + 2)(x + 3)$

$= x(x + 3) + 2(x + 3)$

$= x \times x + x \times 3 + 2 \times x + 2 \times 3$

$= x^2 + \underbrace{3x + 2x}_{\text{Like terms}} + 6$

$= x^2 + 5x + 6$

9 $(3x - 2)^2$

$= (3x - 2)(3x - 2)$

$= 3x(3x - 2) - 2(3x - 2)$

$= 3x \times 3x + 3x \times -2 - 2 \times 3x - 2 \times -2$

$= 9x^2 \underbrace{- 6x - 6x}_{\text{Like terms}} + 4$

$= 9x^2 - 12x + 4$

Factorisation

This is the reverse process to multiplying out brackets. An expression is rewritten with a bracket by taking out the highest factor common to all the terms in the expression.

Examples...

1 $4x + 6 = 2(2x + 3)$

… as **2** is the highest factor common to both **4** and **6**

2 $4x - 12y = 4(x - 3y)$

… as **4** is the highest factor common to both **4** and **12**

3 $3x^2 + 8x = x(3x + 8)$

… as x is the highest factor common to both x^2 and x

4 $6x^2 + 8x = 2x(3x + 4)$

… as **2** is the highest common factor of both **6** and **8** and x is the highest common factor of both x^2 and x

Solving Linear Equations 1

Equations such as…

$$4x = 12$$
$$x + 3 = 7$$
$$2(x + 5) = 14$$

… are all examples of linear equations since the highest power they contain is x^1 (i.e. x). Each of these linear equations can be solved to find the 'unknown' value of x by collecting all the x's on one side and all the numbers on the other side. The simplest linear equation would involve one operation to solve it. Most however require at least two operations.

Examples…

1

$$6x = 18$$
$$\frac{6x}{6} = \frac{18}{6}$$
$$x = 3$$

- Divide both sides of the equation by **6** to leave just x on the left-hand side.

2

$$3x - 5 = 19$$
$$3x - 5 + 5 = 19 + 5$$
$$\frac{3x}{3} = \frac{24}{3}$$
$$x = 8$$

- Add **5** to both sides of the equation to remove the **-5** from the left-hand side.
- Divide both sides of the equation by **3** to leave just x on the left-hand side.

3

$$18 = 4(x + 3)$$
$$18 = 4x + 12$$
$$18 - 12 = 4x + 12 - 12$$
$$\frac{6}{4} = \frac{4x}{4}$$
$$1.5 = x$$
$$\text{or } x = 1.5$$

- Multiply out the bracket on the right-hand side.
- Subtract **12** from both sides of the equation to remove the **+12** on the right-hand side.
- Divide both sides of the equation by **4** to leave just x on the right-hand side.

4

$$18 = 4(x + 9)$$
$$18 = 4x + 36$$
$$18 - 36 = 4x + 36 - 36$$
$$\frac{-18}{4} = \frac{4x}{4}$$
$$-4.5 = x$$
$$\text{or } x = -4.5$$

- Multiply out the bracket on the right-hand side.
- Subtract **36** from both sides of the equation to remove the **+36** on the right-hand side.
- Divide both sides of the equation by **4** to leave just x on the right-hand side.

5

$$5(x + 6) = 20$$
$$5x + 30 = 20$$
$$5x + 30 - 30 = 20 - 30$$
$$\frac{5x}{5} = \frac{-10}{5}$$
$$x = -2$$

- Multiply out the bracket on the left-hand side.
- Subtract **30** from both sides of the equation to remove the **+30** on the left-hand side.
- Divide both sides of the equation by **5** to leave just x on the left-hand side.

Solving Linear Equations 2

The following examples have the 'unknown', e.g. x, appearing on both sides of the equation. Once again they are solved by collecting all the x's on one side and all the numbers on the other side.

It does not really matter on which side of the equal sign you collect all the x's, it is your choice. In the examples below, they are collected on the side that has the most positive x's to start with. This ensures you end up with a value for x rather than $-x$.

Examples...

①
$$8x - 7 = 5x + 2$$
$$8x - 5x - 7 = \cancel{5x} - \cancel{5x} + 2$$
$$3x - \cancel{7} + \cancel{7} = 2 + 7$$
$$\frac{\cancel{3}x}{\cancel{3}} = \frac{9}{3}$$
$$x = 3$$

- Subtract **5x** from both sides of the equation to leave all the x's on the left-hand side.
- Add **7** to both sides of the equation to remove the **-7** on the left-hand side.
- Divide both sides of the equation by **3** to leave just x on the left-hand side.

②
$$4(3x - 2) = 14x + 4$$
$$12x - 8 = 14x + 4$$
$$\cancel{12x} - \cancel{12x} - 8 = 14x - 12x + 4$$
$$-8 - 4 = 2x + \cancel{4} - \cancel{4}$$
$$\frac{-12}{2} = \frac{\cancel{2}x}{\cancel{2}}$$
$$-6 = x$$
$$\text{or } x = -6$$

- Multiply out the bracket on the left-hand side.
- Subtract **12x** from both sides of the equation to leave all the x's on the right-hand side.
- Subtract **4** from both sides of the equation to remove the **+4** on the right-hand side.
- Divide both sides of the equation by **2** to leave just x on the right-hand side.

Problem Solving Using Linear Equations

This involves being given information, forming a linear equation from the information given and then solving the equation.

Example...

The four angles of a quadrilateral are: **a, a + 20°, a + 40° and a + 60°**. Calculate the size of each angle.

Firstly ... we know that the angles of a quadrilateral add up to **360°**. Therefore...

$$a + (a + 20) + (a + 40) + (a + 60) = 360$$
$$4a + 120 = 360$$
$$4a = 240 \quad \longleftarrow \boxed{\text{Subtract 120 from both sides}}$$
$$a = 60° \quad \longleftarrow \boxed{\text{Divide both sides by 4}}$$

$a = 60°$, $a + 20° = 80°$, $a + 40° = 100°$, $a + 60° = 120°$.

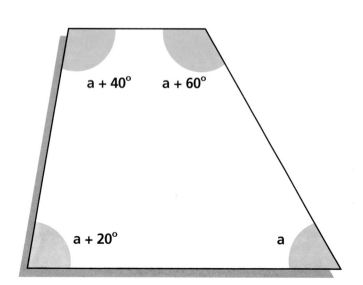

Formulae show the relationship between two or more changeable quantities (variables). They can be written in words, but most often symbols are used instead. For example, the area of a circle is given by the formula: $A = \pi r^2$, which describes the relationship between the area of a circle and its radius.

You can rearrange formulae to make a different letter the 'subject' of the formula, e.g. $a = b + c$ has a as the subject since it is on one side by itself. If we wanted to make b or c the subject then we would need to rearrange the formula by moving terms from one side of the equal sign to the other. The processes involved are the same as solving linear equations (see previous two pages).

Examples...

① Make **b** the subject of the following formula. $a = b + c$ $a - c = b + \cancel{c} - \cancel{c}$ or $b = a - c$	- SUBTRACT **c** from both sides of the formula. This will remove the **+c** on the right-hand side to leave **b** on its own. - REWRITE the formula with **b** on the left-hand side.
② Make **y** the subject of the following formula. $x + y = 7$ $\cancel{x} - \cancel{x} + y = 7 - x$ or $y = -x + 7$	- SUBTRACT **x** from both sides of the formula to remove the **x** on the left-hand side.
③ Make **x** the subject of the following formula. $4(3x + 2y) = 10$ $4 \times 3x + 4 \times 2y = 10$ $12x + 8y = 10$ $12x + \cancel{8y} - \cancel{8y} = 10 - 8y$ $\dfrac{\cancel{12}x}{\cancel{12}} = \dfrac{10 - 8y}{12}$ $x = \dfrac{10 - 8y}{12}$	- MULTIPLY out the bracket on the left-hand side. - SUBTRACT **8y** from both sides of the formula to remove the **+8y** on the left-hand side. - DIVIDE both sides of the formula by **12** to leave just **x** on the left-hand side.
④ Make **r** the subject of the following formula. $A = \pi r^2$ $\dfrac{A}{\pi} = \dfrac{\cancel{\pi} r^2}{\cancel{\pi}}$ $\sqrt{\dfrac{A}{\pi}} = \sqrt{r^{\cancel{2}}}$ $\sqrt{\dfrac{A}{\pi}} = r$ or $r = \sqrt{\dfrac{A}{\pi}}$	- DIVIDE both sides of the formula by π to remove the π on the right-hand side. - Take the SQUARE ROOT of both sides of the formula to remove the 'square' and leave just **r** on the right-hand side. - REWRITE the formula with **r** on the left-hand side.

Formulae 2

Using Formulae

Examples...

1 A company hires a temporary member of staff. If the temp works 32 hours at a rate per hour of £6, calculate the cost of hiring using the following formula:

wage earned = hours worked x rate per hour

Our formula is:

wage earned

= **hours worked x rate per hour**

= **32 hours x £6**

= **£192**

> All we have to do is substitute values into our formula.

---

2 The formula that converts a temperature reading from degrees Celsius (°C) into degrees Fahrenheit (°F) is: $F = \frac{9}{5}C + 32$
What is the temperature in degrees Fahrenheit if the temperature in degrees Celsius is 25°C?

Our formula is: $F = \frac{9}{5}C + 32$

$F = \frac{9}{5} \times 25 + 32$

$F = 45 + 32$

$F = 77°F$

> We now substitute into our formula a value for **C**, which is 25°C, to work out **F**

---

3 The area of a triangle is given by the formula:

$$A = \frac{B \times H}{2}$$

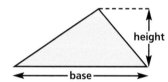

height

base

where **B** is length of base and **H** is height of triangle. Calculate the area of a triangle of height 6cm if the length of its base is 10cm.

Our formula is:

$$A = \frac{B \times H}{2}$$

$$= \frac{10cm \times 6cm}{2}$$

$$= \frac{60}{2}$$

$$= 30cm^2$$

> All we need to do is substitute values for **B** and **H** into our formula.

Deriving Formulae

This means deriving a formula from given information. You may then need to use this formula to work out an unknown quantity. For example...

Derive a formula for the perimeter of a rectangle in terms of its area, **A**, and width, **w**, only. Use it to work out the perimeter if area = 40cm² and width = 4cm

$\ell = \frac{A}{w}$

Perimeter = 2ℓ + 2w

width (w)

Length (ℓ)

Perimeter = 2ℓ + 2w

$= 2\frac{A}{w} + 2w$

$= \frac{2A}{w} + 2w$

$= \frac{2 \times 40}{4} + 2 \times 4$

$= \frac{80}{4} + 8$

$= 20 + 8$

$= 28cm$

> Firstly, we need to substitute $\frac{A}{w}$ for ℓ in our formula for perimeter, to give us the formula in terms of area and width only. All we do then is substitute in values for **A** and **w** to find the perimeter.

Trial and Improvement

This method can be used to find a solution to any equation. As the name suggests we trial a possible solution by substituting its value into the equation.

The process is then repeated using a different possible solution and so on. The idea is that each subsequent attempt is an improvement on the previous attempt.

Examples...

1 The equation $x^2 - 2x = 18$ has a solution somewhere between $x = 5$ and $x = 6$. By trial and improvement, calculate a solution to the equation to 1 decimal place.

Since we are told there is a solution between $x = 5$ and $x = 6$, we will substitute each of these values into the equation in turn to see what $x^2 - 2x$ gives us. Remember, we want to find x when $x^2 - 2x = 18$.

x	$x^2 - 2x$	Comment
5	$5^2 - (2 \times 5) = 25 - 10 = \mathbf{15}$	Less than 18
6	$6^2 - (2 \times 6) = 36 - 12 = \mathbf{24}$	More than 18
Try 5.5	$5.5^2 - (2 \times 5.5) = 30.25 - 11 = \mathbf{19.25}$	More than 18
Try 5.4	$5.4^2 - (2 \times 5.4) = 29.16 - 10.8 = \mathbf{18.36}$	More than 18
Try 5.3	$5.3^2 - (2 \times 5.3) = 28.09 - 10.6 = \mathbf{17.49}$	Less than 18
Try 5.35	$5.35^2 - (2 \times 5.35) = 28.6225 - 10.7 = \mathbf{17.9225}$	Just less than 18

So $x = \mathbf{5.4}$ (to 1 d.p.) since the last trial of 5.35 is less than 18. If the last trial had been more than 18 then the solution would have been $x = \mathbf{5.3}$ (to 1 d.p.). It is important to try the middle value (5.35) to be sure.

. . . .

2 Using trial and improvement, calculate the solution to the equation $x^3 + x = 37$ to 2 decimal places.

With this equation you are given no hints to the value of x, so you must make a 'guestimate' to start.

x	$x^3 + x$	Comment
Try 3	$3^3 + 3 = 27 + 3 = \mathbf{30}$	Less than 37
Try 4	$4^3 + 4 = 64 + 4 = \mathbf{68}$	More than 37
Try 3.5	$3.5^3 + 3.5 = 42.875 + 3.5 = \mathbf{46.375}$	More than 37
Try 3.4	$3.4^3 + 3.4 = 39.304 + 3.4 = \mathbf{42.704}$	More than 37
Try 3.3	$3.3^3 + 3.3 = 35.937 + 3.3 = \mathbf{39.237}$	More than 37
Try 3.2	$3.2^3 + 3.2 = 32.768 + 3.2 = \mathbf{35.968}$	Less than 37
Try 3.25	$3.25^3 + 3.25 = 34.328125 + 3.25 = \mathbf{37.578125}$	More than 37
Try 3.24	$3.24^3 + 3.24 = 34.012224 + 3.24 = \mathbf{37.252224}$	More than 37
Try 3.23	$3.23^3 + 3.23 = 33.698267 + 3.23 = \mathbf{36.928267}$	Less than 37
Try 3.235	$3.235^3 + 3.235 = 33.85500288 + 3.235 = \mathbf{37.090}$	Just more than 37

So $x = \mathbf{3.23}$ (to 2 d.p.) since the final trial was slightly more than 37. If the final trial had been less than 37 then the solution would be $x = \mathbf{3.24}$ (to 2 d.p.). Remember to try the middle value (3.235).

Number Patterns & Sequences 1

A number pattern or sequence is a series of numbers which follow a rule. Each number in a sequence is called a **term**, where the first number in the sequence is called the **1st term** and so on.

| 1st term | 2nd term | 3rd term | 4th term | | The next two terms |

The rule is that each term is **4 more** than the previous term. These terms have a common difference of +4

The rule is that each term is **3 less** than the previous term. These terms have a common difference of -3

The rule is that each term is **3 times** the previous term. These terms don't have a common difference between them

A sequence can also be a series of diagrams.

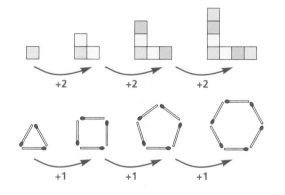

Each diagram (term) has **2 more** boxes in it than the previous diagram. These diagrams have a common difference of +2

Each diagram (term) has **1 more** match in it than the previous diagram. These diagrams have a common difference of +1

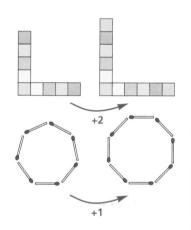

Other Examples...

1 Squared integers

1,   **4,**   **9,**   **16,...**

$(1^2 = 1)$ $(2^2 = 4)$ $(3^2 = 9)$ $(4^2 = 16)$

2 Triangular numbers

1,   **3,**   **6,**   **10,...**
+2   +3   +4

3 Powers of 2

1,   **2,**   **4,**   **8, ...**

$(2^0 = 1)$ $(2^1 = 2)$ $(2^2 = 4)$ $(2^3 = 8)$

4 Powers of 10

1,   **10,**   **100,**   **1000,...**

$(10^0 = 1)$ $(10^1 = 10)$ $(10^2 = 100)$ $(10^3 = 1000)$

Number Patterns & Sequences 2

The nth Term of a Sequence

The nth term is a formula which enables us to generate any term within a particular sequence. Let our sequence of numbers have an **nth term = 2n + 2** where **n** is the position of the term, i.e. the first term has **n = 1**, the second term has **n = 2** and so on. This formula now enables us to generate any term simply by substituting our value for **n** into the formula.

$$\text{nth term} = 2n + 2$$
$$\text{1st term} = 2 \times 1 + 2 = 4$$
$$\text{2nd term} = 2 \times 2 + 2 = 6$$
$$\text{3rd term} = 2 \times 3 + 2 = 8$$
$$\text{4th term} = 2 \times 4 + 2 = 10$$
$$\text{100th term} = 2 \times 100 + 2 = 202$$

So our sequence of numbers would look like…

4, 6, 8, 10, …

Finding the nth Term of an Arithmetic Sequence

A sequence where there is a common difference between the terms can be described by a linear algebraic expression. The general formula for the nth term of these sequences is…

$$\text{nth term} = an + b$$

where **a** is the common difference between the terms and **b** is an integer. The first thing you do is determine the value of **a**. To then find **b** substitute the value for the 1st term, **n=1** and **a** into the formula.

Examples…

❶ **5,   7,   9,   11,…**
   +2   +2   +2

These terms have a common difference of **+2** and so **a = 2**. If we take the 1st term then **n = 1** and it has a value of **5**. We then substitute these values into the formula…

$$\text{nth term} = an + b$$
$$5 = 2 \times 1 + b$$

… to give us **b = 5 - 2 = 3**

… Therefore **nth term = 2n + 3**

… To check **2nd term** = $2 \times 2 + 3 = 4 + 3 = 7$ ✓
          3rd term = $2 \times 3 + 3 = 6 + 3 = 9$ ✓

❷ **20,   17,   14,   11,…**
    -3   -3   -3

These terms have a common difference of **-3** and so **a = -3**. If we take the 1st term then **n = 1** and it has a value of **20**. We then substitute these values into the formula…

$$\text{nth term} = an + b$$
$$20 = -3 \times 1 + b$$

… to give us **b = 20 + 3 = 23**

… Therefore **nth term = -3n + 23**

… To check **2nd term** = $-3 \times 2 + 23 = -6 + 23 = 17$ ✓
          3rd term = $-3 \times 3 + 23 = -9 + 23 = 14$ ✓

Plotting Points

All points are plotted on graph or squared paper. Usually your graph or squared paper is divided into four sections called **quadrants** by two lines known as the **x-axis**, which is a horizontal line, and the **y-axis**, which is a vertical line. The point where the two axes cross is called the **origin** (0,0).

The position of any plotted point is given by its **coordinates**. All coordinates are written as two numbers in a bracket separated by a comma, e.g. (3,4) (5,-2), where…

- The first number represents the **x** coordinate which is read going across horizontally to the right or left.
- The second number represents the **y** coordinate which is read vertically going up or down.

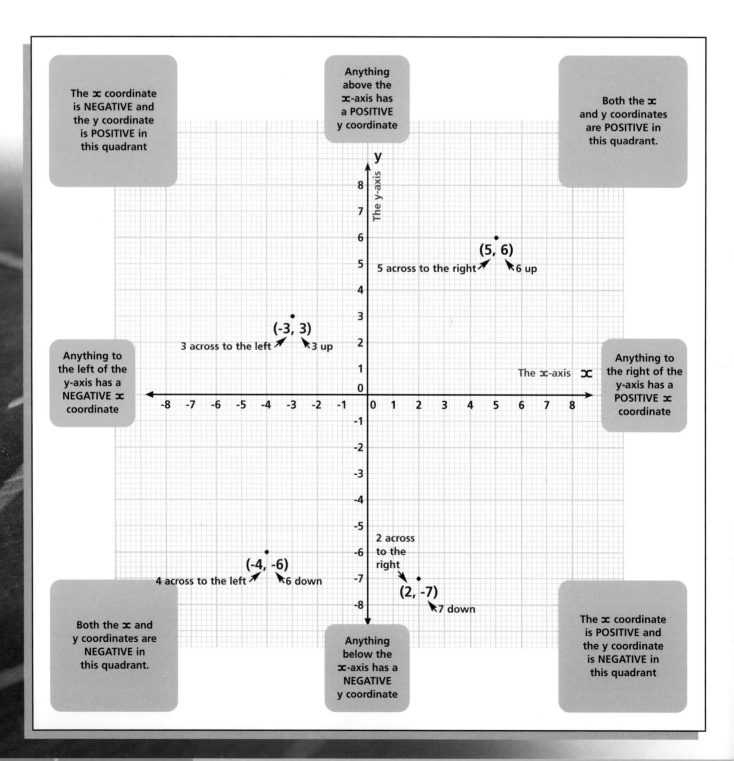

The **x** coordinate is NEGATIVE and the y coordinate is POSITIVE in this quadrant

Anything above the **x**-axis has a POSITIVE y coordinate

Both the **x** and y coordinates are POSITIVE in this quadrant.

(5, 6)
5 across to the right ↗ ↖ 6 up

(-3, 3)
3 across to the left ↗ ↖ 3 up

Anything to the left of the y-axis has a NEGATIVE **x** coordinate

The **x**-axis **x**

Anything to the right of the y-axis has a POSITIVE **x** coordinate

2 across to the right ↓

(-4, -6)
4 across to the left ↗ ↖ 6 down

(2, -7)
↖ 7 down

Both the **x** and y coordinates are NEGATIVE in this quadrant.

Anything below the **x**-axis has a NEGATIVE y coordinate

The **x** coordinate is POSITIVE and the y coordinate is NEGATIVE in this quadrant

Graphs of Linear Functions 1

A linear function, e.g. **y = x, y = 2x - 1, y = 0.5x + 1** (i.e. a function in which the highest power of **x** is **x¹**), will always give you a straight line graph when drawn. To draw the graph of a linear function you only need to plot three points.

Your straight line must pass through all 3 points! If it doesn't then one of your points is wrong. You can either check your table again or better still work out the coordinates of another point.

Examples...

① Draw the graph of **y = 2x - 1** for values of **x** between **-2** and **2**.

Firstly, we need to pick 3 values of **x** within the range, so that we can work out their **y** values. The two extreme values of **x** and one in the middle will do. Make up a table of results as follows:

Table of results for y = 2x - 1

x	-2	0	2
2x	(2 x -2 =) -4	(2 x 0 =) 0	(2 x 2 =) 4
-1	-1	-1	-1
y = 2x - 1	(-4 - 1 =) **-5**	(0 - 1 =) **-1**	(4 - 1 =) **3**

We now have the coordinates of 3 points: (-2,-5), (0,-1) and (2,3) and can plot our graph.

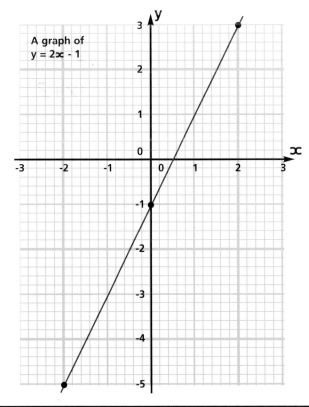

A graph of
y = 2x - 1

② Draw the graph of **2y + x = 4** for values of **x** between **-2** and **2**.

The first thing we have to do is rearrange the function to make **y** the subject. When we have done that we can make up a table of results.

$$2y + x = 4$$
$$2y + x - x = -x + 4 \quad \text{Subtract x from both sides}$$
$$\frac{2y}{2} = \frac{-x}{2} + \frac{4}{2} \quad \text{Divide both sides by 2}$$

To give us ... **y = -0.5x + 2**

Table of results for y = -0.5x + 2

x	-2	0	2
-0.5x	(-0.5 x -2 =) 1	(-0.5 x 0 =) 0	(-0.5 x 2 =) -1
+ 2	+ 2	+ 2	+ 2
y = 0.5x + 2	(1 + 2 =) **3**	(0 + 2 =) **2**	(-1 + 2 =) **1**

We now have the coordinates of 3 points: (-2,3), (0,2) and (2,1) and can plot our graph.

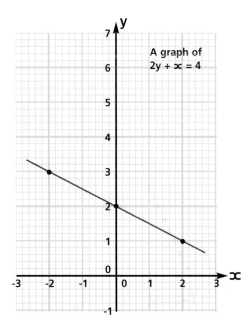

A graph of
2y + x = 4

Graphs of Linear Functions 2

You may also be asked to plot the graph of a linear function where the first thing you have to do is rearrange the function to make **y** the subject. When you have done that you can then make up a table of results and plot your graph.

Examples...

1 Draw the graph of y - 2x = 1 for values of x between -2 and 2.

$$y - 2x = 1$$
$$y - 2x + 2x = 1 + 2x$$
$$y = 2x + 1$$

> Add 2x to both sides to leave just y on the left-hand side

Table of results for y = 2x + 1

x	-2	0	2
2x	(2 x -2 =) -4	(2 x 0 =) 0	(2 x 2 =) 4
+1	+1	+1	+1
y = 2x + 1	(-4 + 1 =) -3	(0 + 1 =) 1	(4 + 1 =) 5

We now have the coordinates of 3 points: (-2,-3), (0,1) and (2,5) and can plot our graph.

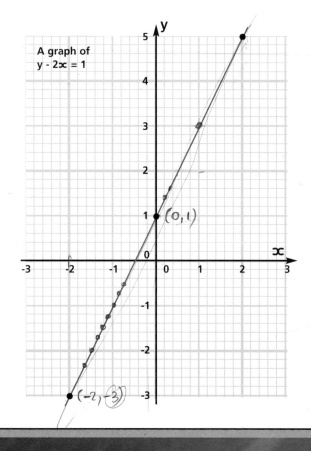

A graph of y - 2x = 1

2 Draw the graph of x + y = 3 for values of x between -2 and 2.

$$x + y = 3$$
$$x - x + y = 3 - x$$
$$y = -x + 3$$

> Subtract x from both sides to leave just y on the left-hand side

Table of results for y = -x + 3

x	-2	0	2
-x	(- -2 =) 2	(-0 =) 0	(-2 =) -2
+ 3	+ 3	+ 3	.+ 3
y = -x + 3	(2 + 3 =) 5	(0 + 3 =) 3	(-2 + 3 =) 1

We now have the coordinates of 3 points: (-2,5), (0,3) and (2,1) and can plot our graph.

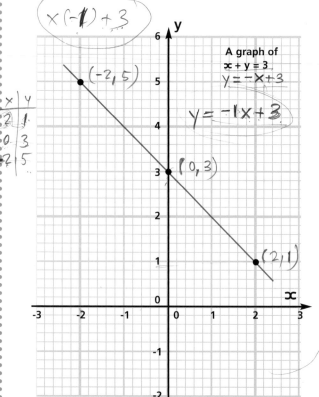

A graph of x + y = 3

Graphs of Linear Functions 3

$y = mx + c$

The general equation for any straight line graph is $y = mx + c$ where…

- … **m** is the value of the gradient. The gradient or slope of a line is a measure of the steepness of the line; the bigger the gradient the steeper the line. The gradient of a line can either be positive or negative, depending on which way the line slopes.
- … **c** is the value of the intercept. The intercept of a line is simply the **y** value at the point where the line crosses the y-axis.

Each of the graphs below has the same intercept (**c = +1**) but a different gradient. The gradients of the lines in graph ❶ and ❷ are both positive with graph ❷ having a steeper slope (**m = 3** as compared to **m = 2** for graph ❶). The line in graph ❸ has a negative gradient (**m = -2**) and so it slopes in the opposite direction to the other two graphs.

Remember, positive (+) gradient goes **up** from left to right (as we read) whereas a negative (-) gradient goes **down** from left to right.

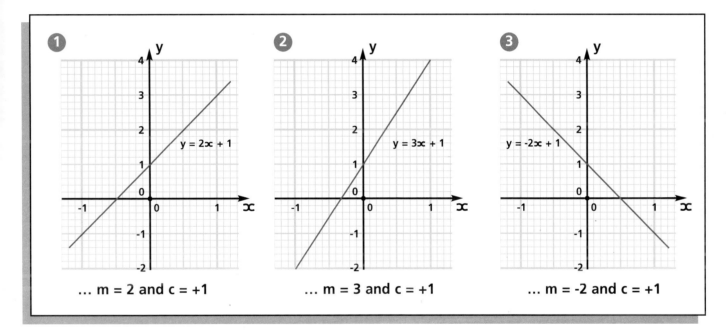

| … m = 2 and c = +1 | … m = 3 and c = +1 | … m = -2 and c = +1 |

Gradients of Parallel Lines

This graph has four lines that are all parallel. This is because each graph has the same gradient (**m = 2**). In other words, lines represented by equations that have the same gradient will be parallel. However, each equation does have a different intercept and so each line crosses the y-axis at a different place.

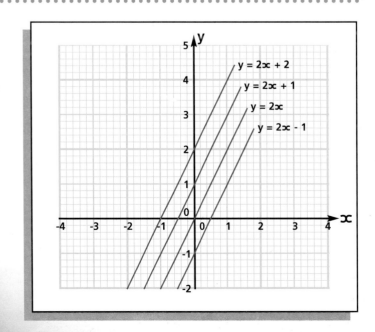

Graphs of Linear Functions 4

Finding the Equation of a Straight Line

In order to find the equation of a straight line graph all you have to do is find the gradient, **m**, and the intercept, **c**. Once you've got values for **m** and **c** you can substitute them into the general equation **y = mx + c** to give the equation of the line. To find the gradient of a line pick two suitable points on your line and then complete a right-angled triangle as shown in the examples below. The gradient is given by the formula:

$$\text{GRADIENT} = \frac{\text{y value}}{\text{x value}}$$ For a positive gradient (see example 1)

$$\text{GRADIENT} = -\frac{\text{y value}}{\text{x value}}$$ For a negative gradient (see example 2)

Remember your measurement for the **y** value and the **x** value must be taken using the scales on the axes. You cannot measure them with a ruler.

Examples...

1

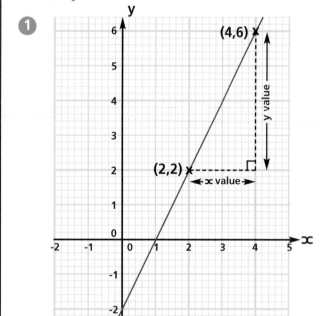

2

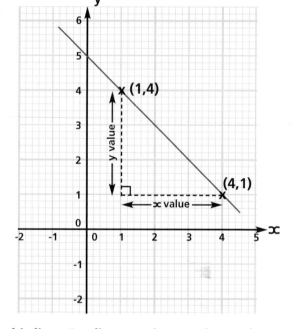

For this line: Gradient, m, is positive and so...

$$m = \frac{\text{y value}}{\text{x value}} = \frac{(6-2)}{(4-2)} = \frac{4}{2} = 2$$

Intercept, c = -2.

The general equation is y = mx + c and so the equation of this line is y = 2x - 2.

For this line: Gradient, m, is negative and so...

$$m = -\frac{\text{y value}}{\text{x value}} = -\frac{(4-1)}{(4-1)} = -\frac{3}{3} = -1$$

Intercept, c = +5.

The general equation is y = mx + c and so the equation of this line is y = -1x + 5 or y = -x + 5.

Lonsdale

Three Special Graphs

❶ Graph of x = 'A NUMBER'

Examples are **x = 4, x = -3, x = 0**. The graphs of these equations are all VERTICAL LINES, i.e. they all go straight up and down.

For the graph **x = 'A NUMBER'** the **x** coordinates of all points on the line are always the same and equal to the 'number'. However, all the points will have different **y** coordinates (see drawn graphs).

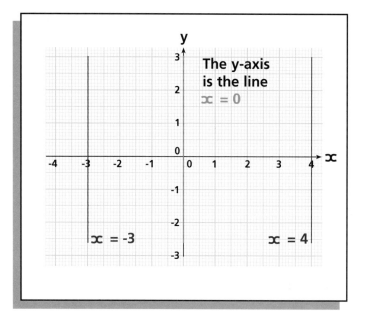

❷ Graph of y = 'A NUMBER'

Examples are **y = 3, y = -2, y = 0**. The graphs of these equations are all HORIZONTAL LINES, i.e. they all go straight across.

For the graph **y = 'A NUMBER'** the **y** coordinates of all points on the line are always the same and equal to the 'number'. This time, however, all the points will have different **x** coordinates (see drawn graphs).

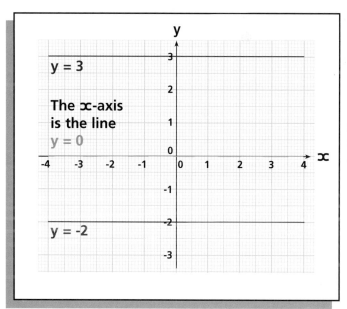

❸ Graph of y = x and y = -x

The graphs of these equations are both DIAGONAL LINES but in opposite directions. Both lines always pass through the origin (0,0) and have a gradient of 1 and -1 respectively.

For the graph **y = x**, the **x** and **y** coordinates of a particular point on the line will be the same numerically and of the same sign (both + or both -).

For the graph **y = -x**, the **x** and **y** coordinates of a particular point on the line will be the same numerically, but of opposite signs.

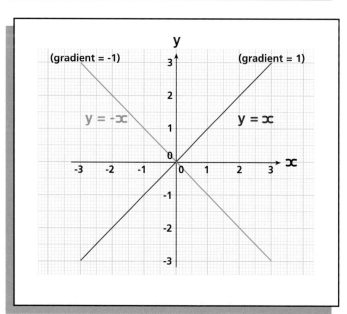

Linear Inequalities 1

The Four Kinds of Inequality

1 **>** **which means 'Greater than'**

e.g. if $x > 4$ then x can have any value 'greater than' **4** but it can't have a value equal to **4**.

This inequality can be shown using a number line. An open ○ circle means that $x = 4$ is not included in the inequality.

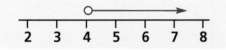

2 **≥** **which means 'Greater than or Equal to'**

e.g. if $x \geq 4$ then x can have any value 'greater than' **4** and its value can also be 'equal to' **4**.

This inequality can be shown using a number line. A closed ● circle means that $x = 4$ is included in the inequality.

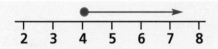

3 **<** **which means 'Less than'**

e.g. if $x < 1$ then x can have any value 'less than' **1** but it can't have a value equal to **1**.

This inequality can be shown using a number line. An open ○ circle means that $x = 1$ is not included in the inequality.

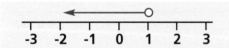

4 **≤** **which means 'Less than or Equal to'**

e.g. if $x \leq 1$ then x can have any value 'less than' **1** and its value can also be 'equal to' **1**

This inequality can be shown using a number line. A closed ● circle means that $x = 1$ is included in the inequality.

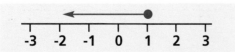

Number lines can also be used to show a combination of inequalities, for example…

1  $-2 \leq x < 5$

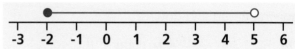

2 $1 < x \leq 4$

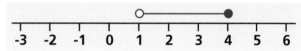

Solving Linear Inequalities

Solving these is just like solving linear equations except we have an inequality sign instead of the equal sign, for example…

1 $x + 2 < 8$

$x + 2 - 2 < 8 - 2$

$x < 6$

2 $3x - 3 \geq x + 7$

$3x - x - 3 \geq x - x + 7$

$2x - 3 + 3 \geq 7 + 3$

$\dfrac{2x}{2} \geq \dfrac{10}{2}$

$x \geq 5$

However, if you multiply or divide an inequality by a negative number then you must always reverse the direction of the inequality sign, for example…

1 $-2x > 6$

$\dfrac{-2x}{-2} < \dfrac{6}{-2}$

$x < -3$

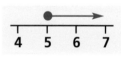

Divide both sides by -2 … inequality sign reverses direction (i.e. > becomes <)

2 $\dfrac{-x}{4} \leq 1.5$

$\dfrac{-x}{4} \times -4 \geq 1.5 \times -4$

$x \geq -6$

Multiply both sides by -4 … inequality sign reverses direction (i.e. ≤ becomes ≥)

Lonsdale

Illustrating Linear Inequalities Graphically

Any linear inequality can be illustrated graphically.
All you have to do is…

1 Treat the inequality as an equation with an equal
(=) sign and draw its graph where a **>** or **<**
inequality is drawn as a dotted line and a
⩾ or **⩽** inequality is drawn as a continuous line.

2 Label and shade in the region which satisfies
the inequality.

Examples…

1 **Illustrate $x < 4$ graphically. Label and
shade the region which satisfies
the inequality.**

- Firstly draw the graph of $x = 4$ (see page 49),
remember to draw a dotted line.

- To find the region which satisfies the
inequality pick two points (we've labelled
them A and B) one on each side of the line
$x = 4$ (see graph).

- Label and shade the region which satisfies
the inequality.

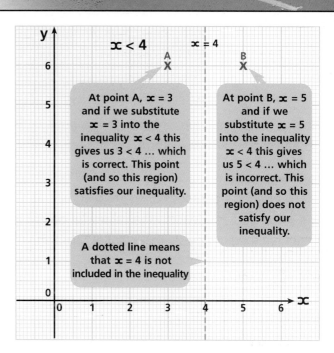

At point A, $x = 3$
and if we substitute
$x = 3$ into the
inequality $x < 4$ this
gives us $3 < 4$ … which
is correct. This point
(and so this region)
satisfies our inequality.

At point B, $x = 5$
and if we
substitute $x = 5$
into the inequality
$x < 4$ this gives
us $5 < 4$ … which
is incorrect. This
point (and so this
region) does not
satisfy our
inequality.

A dotted line means
that $x = 4$ is not
included in the inequality

2 **Illustrate $y ⩾ 3$ graphically. Label and shade
the region that satisfies the inequality.**

- Firstly draw the graph of $y = 3$. Remember to
use a solid line to show that $y = 3$ is included
in the inequality.

- To find the region which satisfies the inequality
pick two points (we've labelled them A and B),
one on each side of the line $y = 3$ (see graph).

- Label and shade the region which satisfies
the inequality.

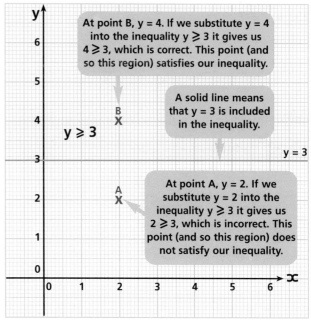

At point B, $y = 4$. If we substitute $y = 4$
into the inequality $y ⩾ 3$ it gives us
$4 ⩾ 3$, which is correct. This point (and
so this region) satisfies our inequality.

A solid line means
that $y = 3$ is included
in the inequality.

At point A, $y = 2$. If we
substitute $y = 2$ into the
inequality $y ⩾ 3$ it gives us
$2 ⩾ 3$, which is incorrect. This
point (and so this region) does
not satisfy our inequality.

If two equations are 'simultaneous', the values for x and y are the same in both equations.

The solution to simultaneous equations can be found by plotting the graphs of the two equations on the same axes and reading the values for x and y where the lines cross. This point is called the **point of intersection**.

Example...

From the graph of the equations $x + y = 5$ and $2x + y = 7$, find values for x and y that satisfy both equations.

- Reading across from the point of intersection
  $y = 3$.

- Reading down from the point of intersection
  $x = 2$.

Substitute these values into both equations to check they are correct.

$x + y = 5$ $2x + y = 7$

$3 + 2 = 5$ ✓ $2 \times 2 + 3 = 7$ ✓

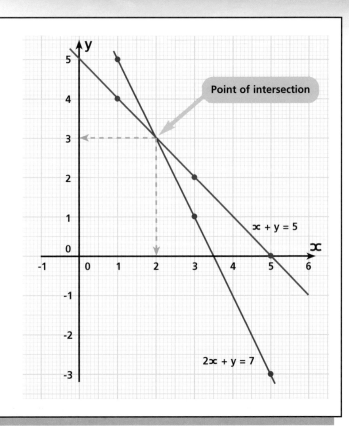

Point of intersection

$x + y = 5$

$2x + y = 7$

Graphs of Quadratic Functions 1

Drawing Graphs of Quadratic Functions

A quadratic function is one in which the highest power is x^2. Examples would include $y = x^2$, $y = x^2 - 5$, $y = x^2 - 2x$, $y = x^2 + 4$. These functions always produce a curved graph such as the ones below. To draw a curved graph we need to plot a **full range of points** as this increases the accuracy of our curve (compare this with straight line graphs).

Examples...

1 Draw the graph of $y = x^2$ for values of x between **-3** and **3** (-3 $\leqslant$ x $\leqslant$ 3).

Table of results for $y = x^2$

x	-3	-2	-1	0	1	2	3
	$(-3)^2=$	$(-2)^2=$	$(-1)^2=$	$(0)^2=$	$(1)^2=$	$(2)^2=$	$(3)^2=$
$y = x^2$	9	4	1	0	1	4	9

We now have the coordinates of 7 points, so we can draw our graph.

Remember... Your curve must be smooth with no wobbly bits in it and it must pass through all of the points plotted.

2 Draw the graph of $y = x^2 - 2x - 2$ for values of x between **-2** and **4** (-2 $\leqslant$ x $\leqslant$ 4).

Table of results for $y = x^2 - 2x - 2$

x	-2	-1	0	1	2	3	4
x^2	$(-2)^2=$ 4	$(-1)^2=$ 1	$(0)^2=$ 0	$(1)^2=$ 1	$(2)^2=$ 4	$(3)^2=$ 9	$(4)^2=$ 16
$-2x$	-2x-2= +4	-2x-1= +2	-2x0= 0	-2x1= -2	-2x2= -4	-2x3= -6	-2x4= -8
-2	-2	-2	-2	-2	-2	-2	-2
$y=x^2-2x-2$	6	1	-2	-3	-2	1	6

Again we have the coordinates of 7 points, so we can draw our graph.

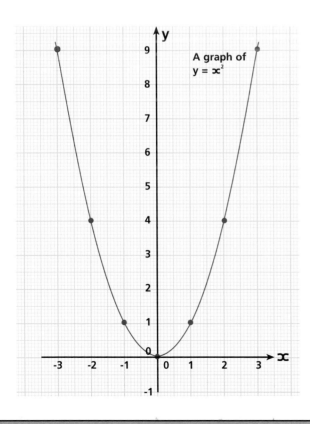

A graph of $y = x^2$

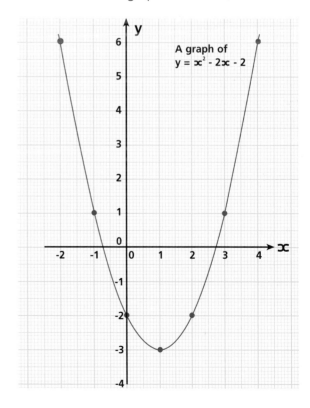

A graph of $y = x^2 - 2x - 2$

Graphs of Quadratic Functions 2

Solving Quadratic Equations Graphically

Graphs of quadratic functions can be used to find approximate solutions to corresponding quadratic equations, for example…

The quadratic equation $x^2 - 2x - 2 = 0$ corresponds with the quadratic function $y = x^2 - 2x - 2$, because $x^2 - 2x - 2$ is common to both. Therefore, the graph of $y = x^2 - 2x - 2$ (see previous page) can be used to find approximate solutions to this equation.

Our quadratic equation is …	$\left(x^2 - 2x - 2\right) = 0$
Our graph is	$y = \left(x^2 - 2x - 2\right)$

You can see that if the equation $x^2 - 2x - 2 = 0$ is substituted into the function, you are left with $y = 0$.

So, to find the approximate solutions you read off the values of x, where the graph crosses the line $y = 0$ (which is the x-axis).

The two approximate solutions to the equation $x^2 - 2x - 2 = 0$ are $x = -0.7$ and $x = 2.7$ (see graph).

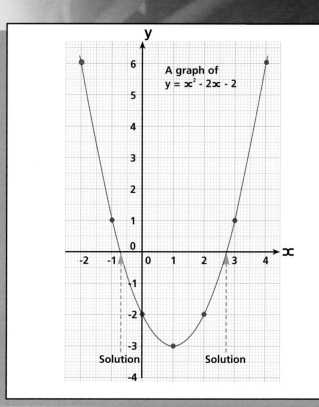

A graph of $y = x^2 - 2x - 2$

Solution   Solution

Graphs of Other Functions

You will not be asked to draw cubic (e.g. $y = x^3$) or reciprocal (e.g. $y = \frac{1}{x}$) graphs, but you will be expected to recognise them.

Cubic Graph

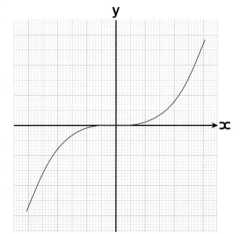

A cubic graph is always a curved graph with a double bend in it.

Reciprocal Graph

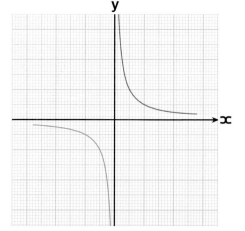

A reciprocal graph always has two separate curves.

Graphs that Describe Real Life Situations

Example...

The table below shows the prices charged by a car hire firm.

Fixed Charge £20
Cost per day £10

Fixed Charge £20
Cost per day £10

a) What is the relationship between cost of hire and number of days hire?

b) Draw a table to show cost of hire up to 7 days and then a graph to show the relationship between cost of hire and number of days hire.

a) Using the information given, the relationship is...

Cost of hire = Fixed charge + (Cost per day x Number of days hire)

If we now substitute our fixed charge and cost per day into the relationship...

Cost of hire (£) = 20 + (10 x Number of days hire)

b) We can now draw a table to show the cost of hire for up to 7 days...

Number of days hire	1	2	3	4	5	6	7
Cost of hire (£) = 20 + (10 x Number of days hire)	20+(10x1)= **30**	20+(10x2)= **40**	20+(10x3)= **50**	20+(10x4)= **60**	20+(10x5)= **70**	20+(10x6)= **80**	20+(10x7)= **90**

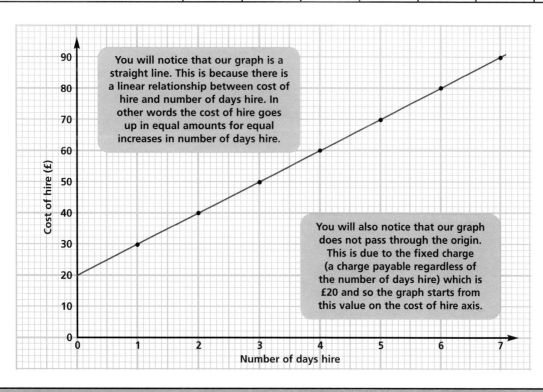

You will notice that our graph is a straight line. This is because there is a linear relationship between cost of hire and number of days hire. In other words the cost of hire goes up in equal amounts for equal increases in number of days hire.

You will also notice that our graph does not pass through the origin. This is due to the fixed charge (a charge payable regardless of the number of days hire) which is £20 and so the graph starts from this value on the cost of hire axis.

Other Graphs 2

Conversion Graphs

These are used to convert values of one quantity into another, e.g. pounds sterling (£) into euros (€) or any other currency, miles into kilometres and so on.

Example

Draw a conversion graph for pounds sterling and euros up to £30 if £1 = €1.60. From your graph convert…

a) £17 into euros

b) €40 into pounds sterling

Before we can draw our graph we need a table of values for pounds sterling and euros.

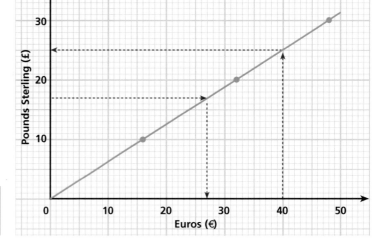

Pounds sterling (£)	10	20	30
Euros (€)	(10x1.6=) **16**	(20x1.6=) **32**	(30x1.6=) **48**

a) Go to £17 on the pounds sterling axis, draw a dotted line across (➡) to the graph and then down (⬇) to the euros axis. **£17 = €27.**

b) Go to €40 on the euros axis, draw a dotted line up (⬆) to the graph and then across (⬅) to the pounds sterling axis. **€40 = £25.**

Other Examples…

Here are 6 other examples (there are numerous others) where a graph can be used to show a real life situation.

All of these graphs require common sense in their interpretation as each one is very different.

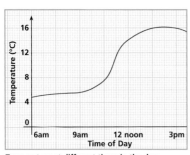

Temperature at different times in the day

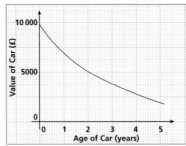

Value of a car as it gets older

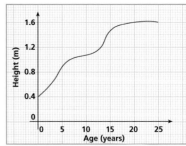

Height of a girl as she gets older

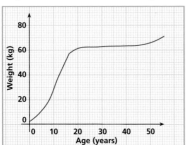

Weight of a man as he gets older

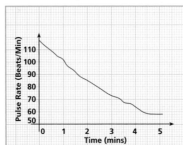

Pulse rate of a runner after the race is over

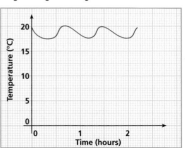

Temperature of a thermostatically controlled room over a period of time

Lonsdale

Distance–time Graphs

These are also known as travel graphs, where distance is always plotted on the vertical axis and time is always plotted on the horizontal axis. For a distance–time graph the slope or gradient is always equal to the speed. If there is no slope, there is no movement, i.e. speed = 0.

Example...

A boy sets off from home riding his bike to go to a friend's house. A distance–time graph of his journey is shown below. Describe his movement between **a)** O and A, **b)** A and B, and **c)** B and C.

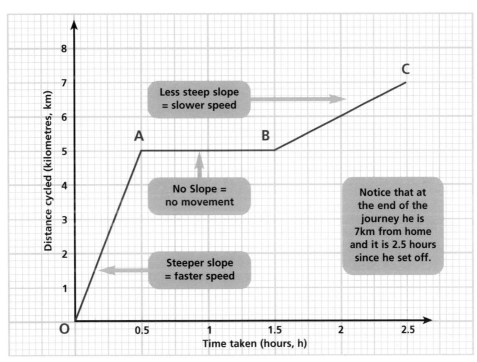

a) Between O and A the boy is cycling with constant speed given by the slope or gradient.

$$\text{Speed} = \frac{\text{Distance}}{\text{Time}}$$

$$= \frac{\text{Distance cycled from O to A}}{\text{Time taken to cycle from O to A}}$$

$$= \frac{5\text{km}}{0.5\text{h}} = 10\text{km/h}$$

b) Between A and B there is no movement, i.e. the boy has stopped cycling for 1 hour.

Speed = 0 since there is no slope or gradient.

c) Between B and C the boy is again cycling with constant speed given by the slope or gradient.

$$\text{Speed} = \frac{\text{Distance}}{\text{Time}}$$

$$= \frac{\text{Distance cycled from B to C}}{\text{Time taken to cycle from B to C}}$$

$$= \frac{2\text{km}}{1\text{h}}$$

$$= 2\text{km/h}$$

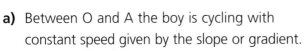

Angles 1

All angles are measured in DEGREES (°). A protractor can be used to measure the size of an angle.

Acute, Right, Obtuse and Reflex Angles

An angle LESS THAN 90° is called an **ACUTE ANGLE**

An angle EQUAL TO 90° is called a **RIGHT ANGLE**

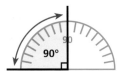 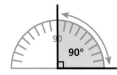

An angle GREATER THAN 90° but LESS THAN 180° is called an **OBTUSE ANGLE**

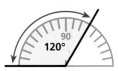 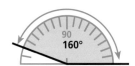

An angle GREATER THAN 180° is called a **REFLEX ANGLE**

 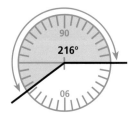

Angles on a Straight Line, at a Point and Vertically Opposite

Angles on a straight line add up to 180° (also known as Adjacent Angles)

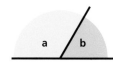

a = 120°
b = 60°   a + b = 180°

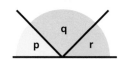

p = 45°
q = 90°   p + q + r = 180°
r = 45°

Angles at a point add up to 360°

a = 240°
b = 120°   a + b = 360°

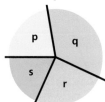

p = 80°
q = 125°
r = 90°   p + q + r + s = 360°
s = 65°

Vertically opposite angles are equal

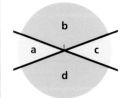

a = 40° } Vertically opposite
c = 40°
b = 140° } Vertically opposite
d = 140°

Examples...

1

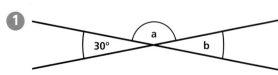

a = 180° - 30° = 150°
(Angles on a straight line add up to 180°)
b = 30° (Vertically opposite angles are equal)

2 **c = 360° - (120° + 160°)**
c = 360° - 280° = 80°
(Angles at a point add up to 360°)

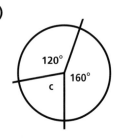

Parallel Lines

Parallel lines run in exactly the same direction and never meet. Parallel lines are shown by arrows on the lines concerned. There is no limit to the number of lines which may run parallel to each other. When a straight line crosses two or more parallel lines, corresponding, alternate and allied angles are formed.

Alternate Angles

- Alternate angles are formed on opposite (alternate) sides of a line which crosses two or more parallel lines.
- Alternate angles are always equal in size.
- Alternate angles can be easily spotted because they form a letter **Z** (although sometimes it may be reversed, **Ƨ**!!).

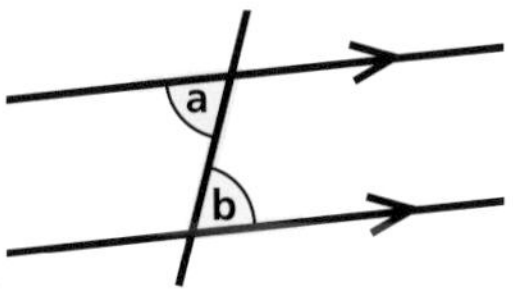

a = 70°, b = 70° } a = b alternate angles

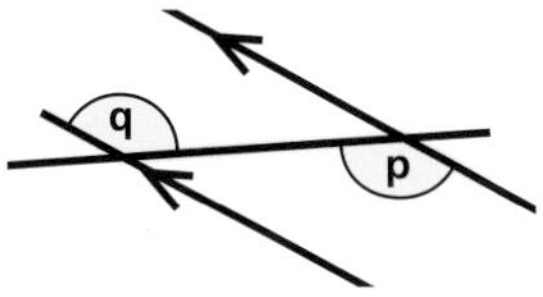

p = 145°, q = 145° } p = q alternate angles

Corresponding Angles

- Corresponding angles are formed on the same side of a line, which crosses two or more parallel lines. They all appear in matching (corresponding) positions above or below the parallel lines.
- Corresponding angles are always equal in size.
- Corresponding angles can be easily spotted because they form a letter **F** (although sometimes it may be reversed, **ꟻ**, or upside down **Ⅎ**, **Ⅎ**!!)

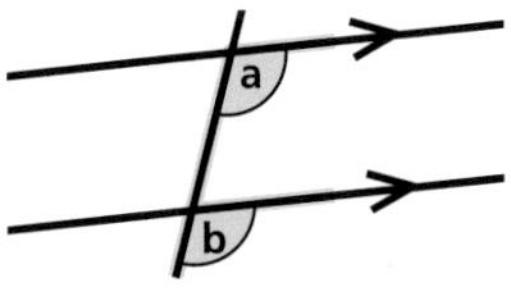

a = 110°, b = 110° } a = b corresponding angles

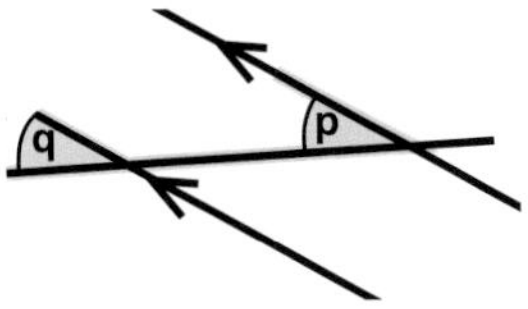

p = 35°, q = 35° } p = q corresponding angles

Co-interior Angles (Allied Angles)

- Co-interior angles are formed on the same side of a line, which crosses two or more parallel lines. They appear inside two parallel lines, facing each other.
- Co-interior angles always add up to 180°.
- Co-interior angles can be easily spotted because they form a letter **⊏** or **⊔** (although sometimes it may be reversed, **⊐** or **⊓**!!).

* Co-interior angles do not appear on the course specification. They are included here because they will help you to understand the relationships between the different angles formed when a straight line crosses two or more parallel lines. You will find them useful when calculating angles too!

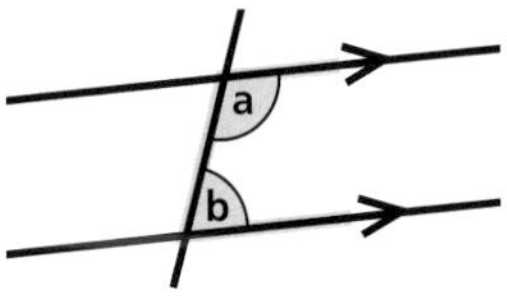

a = 100°, b = 80° } **a + b = 180°** They are co-interior angles

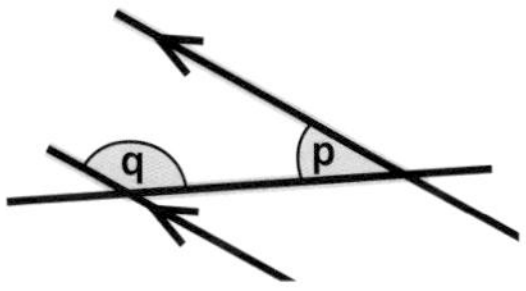

p = 65°, q = 115° } **p + q = 180°** They are co-interior angles

Example

Calculate the angles **a**, **b**, and **c** in relation to x in the following parallelogram.

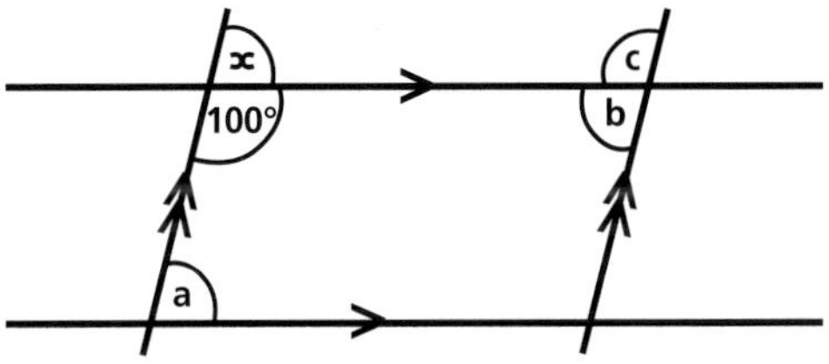

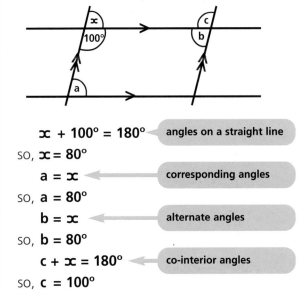

$x + 100° = 180°$ ← **angles on a straight line**

so, $x = 80°$

$a = x$ ← **corresponding angles**

so, $a = 80°$

$b = x$ ← **alternate angles**

so, $b = 80°$

$c + x = 180°$ ← **co-interior angles**

so, $c = 100°$

Triangles

A triangle is a 3-sided two-dimensional shape. The interior angles of the triangle below are **a**, **b** and **c**.

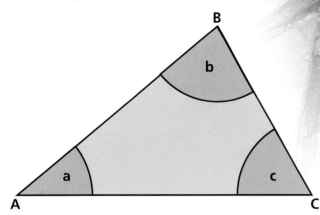

If we extend the side **AC** to point **D**, and add a line from **C** to **E** which runs parallel to **AB** then we get the following diagram.

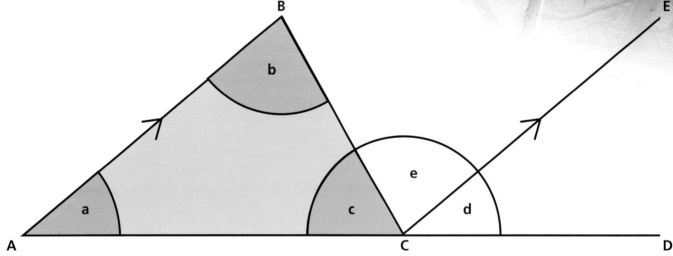

We can now say the following things about these particular angles:

❶ The Interior Angles of a Triangle add up to 180°

From our diagram…

e = b ⟵ alternate angles

d = a ⟵ corresponding angles

However…

c + e + d = 180° ⟵ angles on a straight line add up to 180°

Therefore…

c + b + a = 180°, which proves that…

THE INTERIOR ANGLES OF A TRIANGLE ADD UP TO 180°

❷ The Exterior Angle of a Triangle is equal to the sum of the Interior Angles at the other two vertices

The exterior angle of this triangle at the vertex (corner) C is angle BCD. However we have already shown that:

e = b ⟵ alternate angles

d = a ⟵ corresponding angles

Therefore **d + e = a + b**, which proves that…

THE EXTERIOR ANGLE OF A TRIANGLE IS EQUAL TO THE SUM OF THE INTERIOR ANGLES AT THE OTHER TWO VERTICES.

Types of Triangle

<table>
<tr>
<td>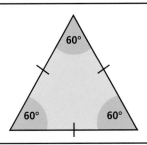</td>
<td>

Right-angled triangles

- One angle is equal to 90°.

</td>
</tr>
<tr>
<td>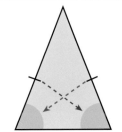</td>
<td>

Equilateral triangles

- All sides are equal in length.
- All the angles are equal to 60°.

</td>
</tr>
<tr>
<td>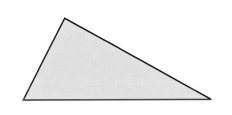</td>
<td>

Isosceles triangles

- Two sides only are equal in length.
- Two angles only are equal in size
  (angles opposite the equal sides).
  These are usually referred to as the base angles.

</td>
</tr>
<tr>
<td></td>
<td>

Scalene triangles

- This is the name given to triangles which
  have no equal sides and no equal angles.

</td>
</tr>
</table>

Example...

The following diagram shows an isosceles and a right-angled triangle. Calculate the angles **a** to **f** explaining your reasoning.

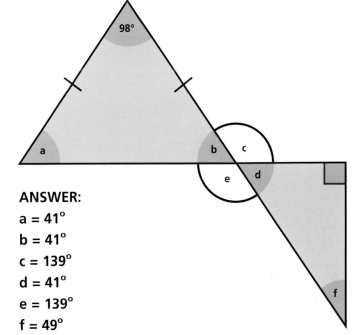

$a = b$ (Base angles of an isosceles triangle)

But, $a + b + 98° = 180°$ (Interior angles of a triangle)

so, $a + b = 82°$ so each one is equal to **41°**.

$b + c = 180°$ (Angles on a straight line)

$c = 180° - 41° = 139°$

$b = d$ (Vertically opposite angles) so, $d = 41°$

$c = e$ (Vertically opposite angles) so, $e = 139°$

$d + f + \text{right-angle} = 180°$

(Interior angles of a triangle)

so, $f = 180° - 90° - 41° = 49°$

ANSWER:

$a = 41°$

$b = 41°$

$c = 139°$

$d = 41°$

$e = 139°$

$f = 49°$

Quadrilaterals

A quadrilateral is a 4-sided, two-dimensional shape which has interior angles that add up to 360°.

Types of Quadrilateral

Square		• All the sides are equal in length • Opposite sides are parallel • All the angles are equal to 90° • Diagonals are equal and bisect each other at right-angles. • Diagonals also bisect each of the interior angles.
Parallelogram		• Opposite sides are equal in length • Opposite sides are parallel • Opposite angles are equal in size • Diagonals bisect each other.
Rhombus		• All the sides are equal in length • Opposite sides are parallel • Opposite angles are equal in size • Diagonals bisect each other at right-angles • Diagonals also bisect the interior angles.
Rectangle		• Opposite sides are equal in length • Opposite sides are parallel • All the angles are equal to 90° • Diagonals are equal and bisect each other.
Trapezium		• No sides equal in length • One pair of sides parallel • No angles equal in size
Kite		• 2 pairs of equal adjacent sides • 1 pair of opposite equal angles • Diagonals cross at right-angles and one bisects the other.

The Interior Angles of a Quadrilateral

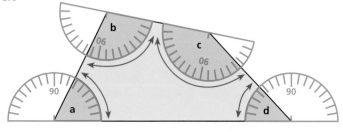

In this quadrilateral…

a = 63°, b = 106°, c = 145°, d = 46°

If we add these together…

63° + 106° + 145° + 46° = 360°

This is true of all quadrilaterals and can be proved by dividing the quadrilateral into 2 triangles:

p + q + r = 180° (Interior angles of a triangle)

s + t + u = 180° (Interior angles of a triangle)

The sum of the interior angles of the quadrilateral is

(p + s) + q + (r + t) + u which is therefore equal to

(p + q + r) + (s + t + u)

i.e. **180° + 180° = 360°**

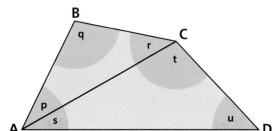

Irregular Polygons

Polygons

A polygon is a two-dimensional shape with 3 or more sides. We have already seen the 3-sided polygon (triangle) and the 4-sided polygon (quadrilateral). A polygon is said to be REGULAR if all its sides and all its angles are equal. Otherwise it is known as an IRREGULAR polygon. Take a look at the two irregular polygons below.

Interior and Exterior Angles of a Polygon

The angles inside a polygon are called the INTERIOR ANGLES and those outside are called the EXTERIOR ANGLES. As for triangles and quadrilaterals the size of each of these angles can be measured using a protractor.

Interior angles	Exterior angles	Interior + Exterior angles
a = 100°	p = 80°	a + p = 180°
b = 100°	q = 80°	b + q = 180°
c = 140°	r = 40°	c + r = 180°
d = 70°	s = 110°	d + s = 180°
e = 130°	t = 50°	e + t = 180°
a+b+c+d+e = 540°	p+q+r+s+t = 360°	

PENTAGON
(5 sided polygon)

Interior angles	Exterior angles	Interior + Exterior angles
a = 121°	p = 59°	a + p = 180°
b = 89°	q = 91°	b + q = 180°
c = 158°	r = 22°	c + r = 180°
d = 136°	s = 44°	d + s = 180°
e = 63°	t = 117°	e + t = 180°
f = 153°	u = 27°	f + u = 180°
a+b+c+d+e+f = 720°	p+q+r+s+t+u = 360°	

HEXAGON
(6 sided polygon)

We can see from above that…

1 The Exterior Angles of a polygon always add up to 360°

2 The Interior Angle + the Exterior Angle always add up to 180°

We can also see that the interior angles of different polygons do not add up to the same number of degrees. A triangle is 180°, a quadrilateral is 360°, a pentagon is 540°, a hexagon is 720°. The more sides the polygon has the greater the sum of the interior angles.

The sum of the interior angles
= (n - 2) x 180°
(where n = number of sides)

Name of Polygon	Number of sides (n)	Sum of Interior Angles, (n - 2) x 180°	Sum of Exterior Angles
Triangle	3	180°	360°
Quadrilateral	4	360°	360°
Pentagon	5	540°	360°
Hexagon	6	720°	360°

Regular Polygons

Regular Polygons

These are polygons that have…

- **Sides of the same length**
- **Interior angles of the same size**
- **Exterior angles of the same size**

Here are four examples of regular polygons:

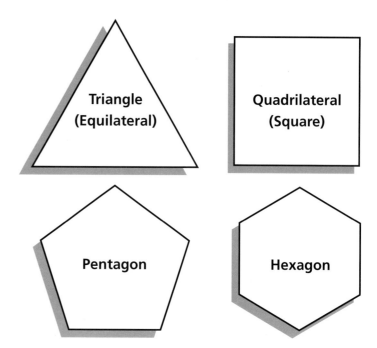

Triangle (Equilateral)

Quadrilateral (Square)

Pentagon

Hexagon

Knowing that the exterior angles of a polygon add up to 360°, that the interior angles are equal in a regular polygon and that the exterior and interior angles add up to 180° enables various calculations to be performed:

Examples…

1 Calculate the size of **a)** each exterior, and **b)** each interior angle for a regular hexagon (6 sides).

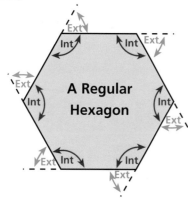

A Regular Hexagon

A Regular Hexagon has 6 equal Interior angles and 6 equal Exterior angles.

a) The Exterior angles of a Hexagon add up to 360° (see previous page)

Each Exterior Angle = $\frac{360°}{6}$ = 60°

b) The Interior angle + the Exterior angle add up to 180° (see previous page)

Each Interior Angle
= 180° - Exterior Angle
= 180° - 60° = 120°

2 A regular polygon has each interior angle = 108°. Calculate **a)** the size of each exterior angle, and **b)** the number of sides the polygon has.

a) The Interior angle + the Exterior angle add up to 180°.

Each Exterior Angle
= 180° - Interior Angle
= 180° - 108° = 72°

b) The Exterior angles of a Polygon add up to 360° (see previous page)

Number of Exterior Angles = $\frac{360°}{72°}$ = 5

Number of sides = 5
(i.e. it is a regular PENTAGON)

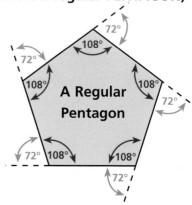

A Regular Pentagon

Congruence and Tessellation

Congruent Shapes

These boys are IDENTICAL in their SIZE and SHAPE although their position relative to each other may be different. These four boys are congruent:

These four shapes are congruent:

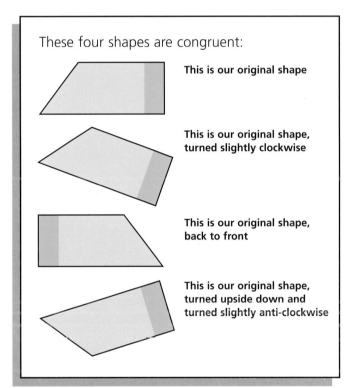

This is our original shape

This is our original shape, turned slightly clockwise

This is our original shape, back to front

This is our original shape, turned upside down and turned slightly anti-clockwise

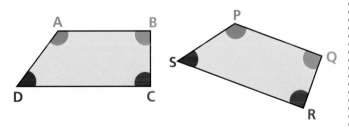

Shape ABCD and shape PQRS are CONGRUENT because $\hat{A} = \hat{P}$, $\hat{B} = \hat{Q}$, $\hat{C} = \hat{R}$ and $\hat{D} = \hat{S}$

TWO CONGRUENT SHAPES HAVE ANGLES THE SAME SIZE and also AB = PQ, BC = QR, CD = RS and DA = SP

TWO CONGRUENT SHAPES HAVE SIDES OF THE SAME LENGTH

Tessellations

A TESSELLATION is a pattern of CONGRUENT SHAPES that fit together with NO GAPS IN BETWEEN to cover a flat surface. Your kitchen floor may well be a tessellation. Not all congruent shapes form a tessellation.

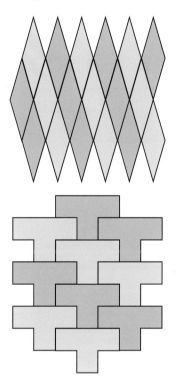

A tessellation can also be made using two or more congruent shapes.

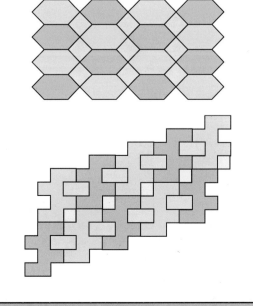

Similarity

Similar Shapes

These boys are IDENTICAL in their SHAPE but they are NOT IDENTICAL in SIZE (they can be bigger or smaller). Yet again their position relative to each other may be different. These four boys are SIMILAR:

These four shapes are similar.

This is our original shape

This is our original shape, but bigger in size.

This is our original shape, but smaller in size.

This is our original shape, smaller in size, upside down and turned slightly clockwise.

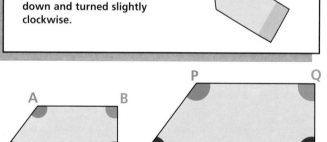

Shape ABCD and shape PQRS are SIMILAR because $\hat{A} = \hat{P}$, $\hat{B} = \hat{Q}$, $\hat{C} = \hat{R}$ and $\hat{D} = \hat{S}$

TWO SIMILAR SHAPES HAVE ANGLES THE SAME SIZE and also $\frac{AB}{PQ} = \frac{BC}{QR} = \frac{CD}{RS} = \frac{DA}{SP}$

or AB:PQ = BC:QR = CD:RS = DA:SP

TWO SIMILAR SHAPES HAVE SIDES WHOSE LENGTH ARE IN THE SAME RATIO.

Any two circles and any two squares are mathematically similar, while **in general**, two rectangles are not.

Example

The two triangles below are similar.
Calculate the length of...
a) QR
b) AC

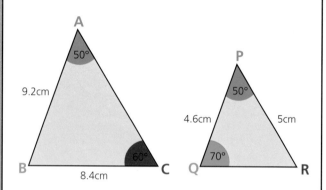

In triangle **ABC**, $\hat{B}$ **= 70°** (180° − (60° + 50°)) and in triangle **PQR**, $\hat{R}$ **= 60°** (180° − (70° + 50°)) And so $\hat{A} = \hat{P}$, $\hat{B} = \hat{Q}$, $\hat{C} = \hat{R}$

This means that triangle **ABC** is similar to triangle **PQR** which means that...

$$\frac{AB}{PQ} = \frac{BC}{QR} = \frac{AC}{PR}$$

> Don't assume that the shapes (in this case triangles) are always lettered in alphabetical order

$$\frac{9.2cm}{4.6cm} = \frac{8.4cm}{QR} = \frac{AC}{5cm}$$

We can now calculate the unknown lengths...

a) $\frac{9.2cm}{4.6cm} = \frac{8.4cm}{QR}$

$QR = \frac{8.4cm \times 4.6cm}{9.2cm}$

> Rearranged to get QR on its own

$QR = \textbf{4.2cm}$

b) $\frac{9.2cm}{4.6cm} = \frac{AC}{5cm}$

$AC = \frac{9.2cm \times 5cm}{4.6cm}$

> Rearranged to get AC on its own

$AC = \textbf{10cm}$

Pythagoras

Pythagoras was a Greek philosopher and mathematician who lived over 2000 years ago. His theorem is used to calculate the length of an unknown side in a right-angled triangle when the lengths of the other two sides are known. The theorem states… **'the square on the Hypotenuse of a right-angled triangle is equal to the sum of the squares on the other two sides'.**

This is shown in our diagram. The square on the hypotenuse (the longest side, always found opposite the right-angle) is 25, which is the sum (16 + 9) of the squares on the other two sides. This can be summarised using the formula $c^2 = a^2 + b^2$. Often, you are asked to work out the length of the hypotenuse (c). In our diagram, we know that $c^2 = \textbf{25 squares}$. So, if you remember powers and roots (pages 14 - 16)… $c^2 = 25$ and so $c = \sqrt{25} = \textbf{5 units}$

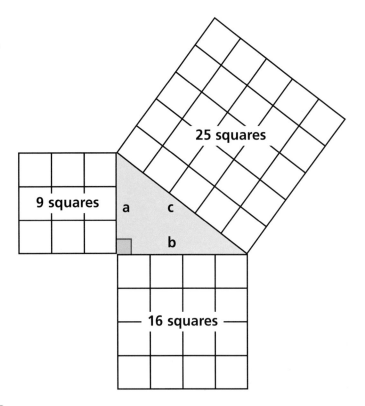

Examples…

1 Calculate the length of **c** in the following right-angled triangle.

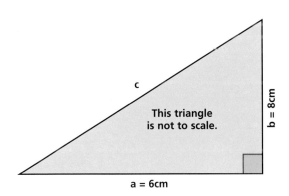

Using Pythagoras' Theorem

$c^2 = a^2 + b^2$

$c^2 = 6^2 + 8^2$

$c^2 = 36 + 64$

$c^2 = 100$

To get **c** we need to take the square root.

$c = \sqrt{100}$

$c = \textbf{10cm}$ (remember the units)

2 Calculate the length of **c** in the following right-angled triangle to 1 decimal place.

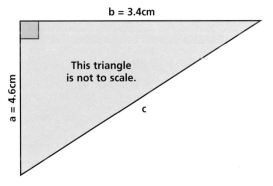

Using Pythagoras' Theorem

$c^2 = a^2 + b^2$

$c^2 = 4.6^2 + 3.4^2$

$c^2 = 21.16 + 11.56$

$c^2 = 32.72$

To get **c** we need to take the square root.

$c = \sqrt{32.72}$

$c = \textbf{5.7cm}$ (remember the units)

Pythagoras' Theorem 2

Using Pythagoras' Theorem to Calculate the Length of One of the Shorter Sides

So far we have used Pythagoras' Theorem to find the square and length of the hypotenuse. It can also be used to calculate the square and length of one of the shorter sides.

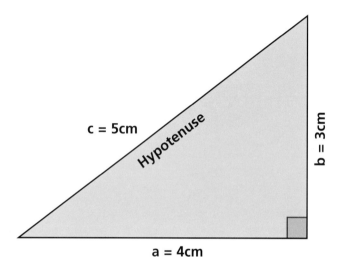

If we look at our formula $c^2 = a^2 + b^2$, it can be rearranged to make a^2 or b^2 the subject:

$$a^2 = c^2 - b^2$$
$$b^2 = c^2 - a^2$$

We can check this works by substituting the side lengths on our diagram into the rearranged formula.

$$a^2 = c^2 - b^2$$
$$4^2 = 5^2 - 3^2$$
$$16 = 25 - 9 \checkmark$$

$$b^2 = c^2 - a^2$$
$$3^2 = 5^2 - 4^2$$
$$9 = 25 - 16 \checkmark$$

The square on one of the shorter sides	=	The square on the Hypotenuse	–	The square on the other short side

Examples...

① Calculate the length of **b** in the following right-angled triangle.

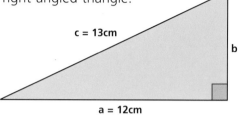

Using Pythagoras' Theorem rearranged.
$$b^2 = c^2 - a^2$$
$$b^2 = 13^2 - 12^2$$
$$b^2 = 169 - 144$$
$$b^2 = 25$$

To get **b** we need to take the square root

$$b = \sqrt{25} = 5cm$$

② Calculate the height of the isosceles triangle shown below, to 3 significant figures.

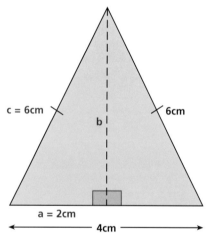

First we must divide the triangle into two right-angled triangles (as shown by the dotted line) in order to use Pythagoras' theorem and label the one we are going to work with (in red).

$$b^2 = c^2 - a^2$$ ← This would be true for either right-angled triangle
$$b^2 = 6^2 - 2^2$$
$$b^2 = 36 - 4$$ ← half the base of the isosceles triangle
$$b^2 = 32$$

To get **b** we need to take the square root

$$b = \sqrt{32} = 5.66cm$$

Transformations 1

Types of Transformation

A transformation is a process which changes the position (and possibly the size and orientation) of a shape. There are four different types of transformation: **reflection**, **rotation**, **translation**, **enlargement**.

① Reflection

A reflection in a line produces a mirror image in which corresponding points on the original shape and the mirror image are always the same distance from the mirror line. A line joining corresponding points always crosses the mirror line at 90°. To describe a reflection you must specify the MIRROR LINE by giving the equation of the line of reflection (in the examples on the right these are $x = 6$ and $y = 1$). As you can see, in a reflection, the ORIENTATION and POSITION changes but everything else stays the same. Therefore the image is congruent to the object under a reflection. Difficult reflections can be completed more easily if you use tracing paper. The example below is a reflection in the line $y = -1$.

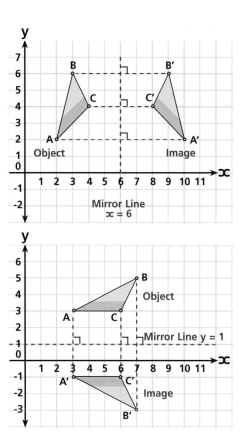

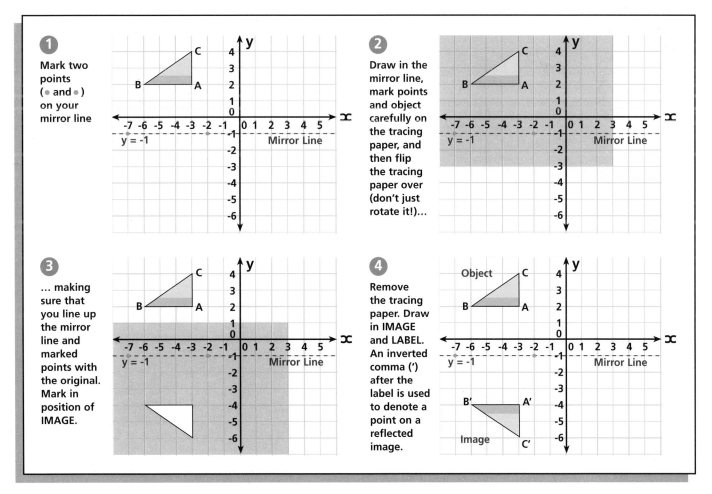

1. **Mark two points (● and ●) on your mirror line**

2. **Draw in the mirror line, mark points and object carefully on the tracing paper, and then flip the tracing paper over (don't just rotate it!)...**

3. **... making sure that you line up the mirror line and marked points with the original. Mark in position of IMAGE.**

4. **Remove the tracing paper. Draw in IMAGE and LABEL. An inverted comma (') after the label is used to denote a point on a reflected image.**

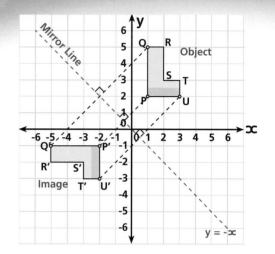

Reflection (cont.)

The equation you are given for the mirror line may produce a diagonal line of reflection, e.g. $y = x$.

Reflections in diagonal lines of reflection are slightly trickier, but if you follow the same basic steps you should not have a problem.

Example

Reflect triangle ABC in the line $y = x$. Label the image A'B'C'.

① Mark two points (● and ●) on your mirror line

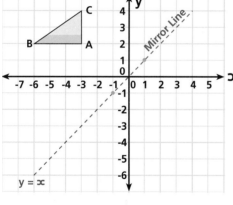

② Draw in the mirror line, mark points and object carefully on the tracing paper, and then flip the tracing paper over (don't just rotate it!)…

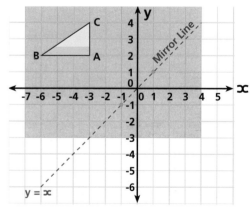

③ … making sure that you line up the mirror line and marked points with the original. Mark in position of IMAGE.

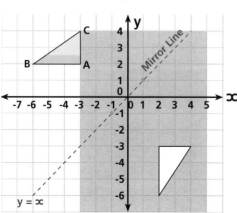

④ Remove the tracing paper. Draw in IMAGE and LABEL. An inverted comma (') after the label is used to denote a point on a reflected image.

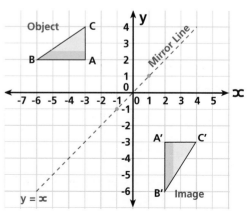

Transformations 3

❷ Rotation

A rotation turns a shape through a clockwise or anti-clockwise angle about a fixed point known as the Centre of Rotation. All lines in the shape rotate through the same angle. Rotation, (just like reflection) changes the ORIENTATION and POSITION of the shape, but everything else stays the same.

Therefore the image is congruent to the object under a rotation. To describe a rotation, you must specify the following three things:
• The DIRECTION OF TURN (clockwise/anti-clockwise)
• The CENTRE OF ROTATION
• The AMOUNT TURNED.

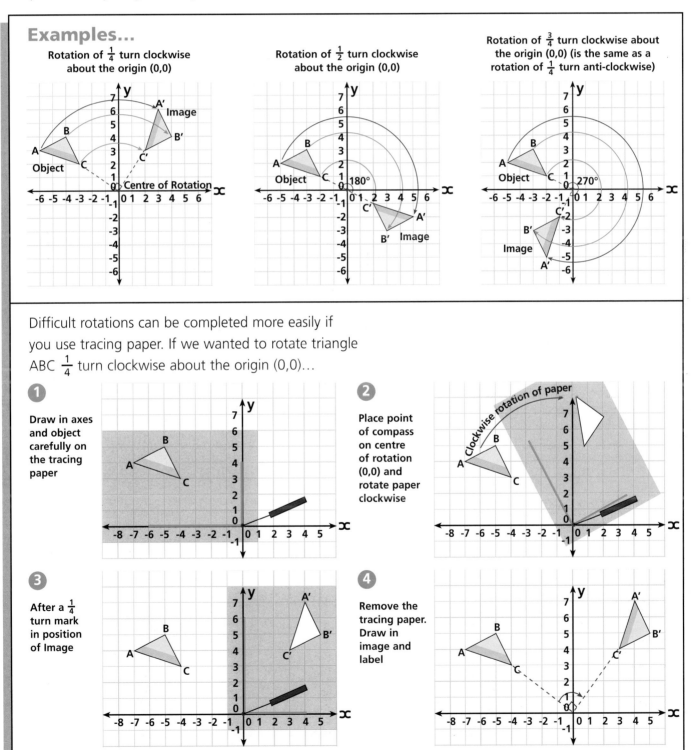

Examples...

Rotation of ¼ turn clockwise about the origin (0,0)

Rotation of ½ turn clockwise about the origin (0,0)

Rotation of ¾ turn clockwise about the origin (0,0) (is the same as a rotation of ¼ turn anti-clockwise)

Difficult rotations can be completed more easily if you use tracing paper. If we wanted to rotate triangle ABC ¼ turn clockwise about the origin (0,0)...

❶ Draw in axes and object carefully on the tracing paper

❷ Place point of compass on centre of rotation (0,0) and rotate paper clockwise

❸ After a ¼ turn mark in position of Image

❹ Remove the tracing paper. Draw in image and label

Transformations 4

❸ Translation

A translation alters the position of a shape by moving every point of it by the same distance in the same direction. To describe a translation, you must specify the following two things:

- THE DIRECTION OF THE MOVEMENT
- THE DISTANCE MOVED

This can be summarised using brackets in which the movement in the **x** direction is placed directly above the movement in the **y** direction. Positive and negative numbers are used to indicate the direction of the movement. (See diagram alongside.) Translation only changes the POSITION of the shape. Everything else stays the same, so that any figure is congruent to its image under a translation.

Difficult translations can be completed more easily if you use tracing paper. Notice that all points (**P'**, **Q'**, **R'**, **S'**, **T'** and **U'**) in the example below have moved 6 to the right and 6 down.

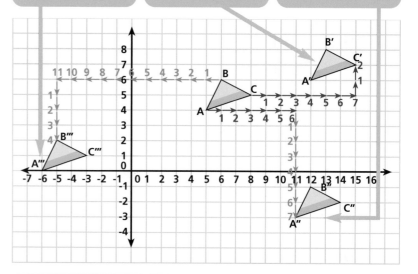

ABC has been translated to A"B"C" by moving 11 squares to the left and then 4 squares down. This translation is written as
$\begin{pmatrix} -11 \\ -4 \end{pmatrix}$

ABC has been translated to A'B'C' by moving 7 squares to the right and then 2 squares up. This translation is written as
$\begin{pmatrix} 7 \\ 2 \end{pmatrix}$

ABC has been translated to A'''B'''C''' by moving 6 squares to the right and then 7 squares down. This translation is written as
$\begin{pmatrix} 6 \\ -7 \end{pmatrix}$

- **Movement to the right (→) or up (↟) is positive**
- Movement to the left (←) or down (↡) is negative

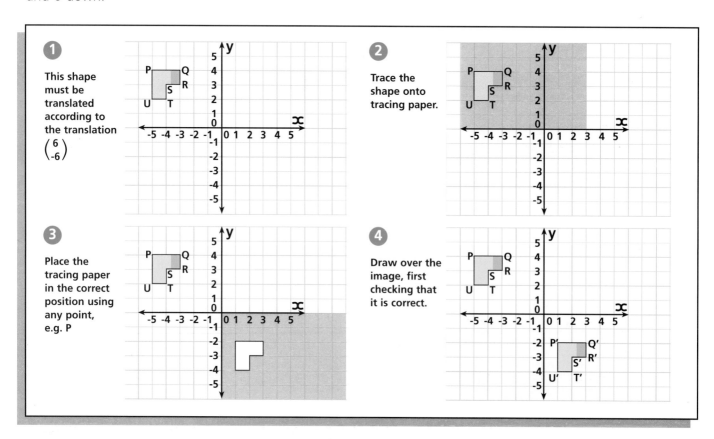

❶ This shape must be translated according to the translation $\begin{pmatrix} 6 \\ -6 \end{pmatrix}$

❷ Trace the shape onto tracing paper.

❸ Place the tracing paper in the correct position using any point, e.g. P

❹ Draw over the image, first checking that it is correct.

Lonsdale

❹ Enlargement

An enlargement changes the size of a shape. The shape can be made bigger or smaller according to the Scale Factor. All enlargements take place from one point called the Centre of Enlargement.

To describe an enlargement you must specify the following two things:
- THE CENTRE OF ENLARGEMENT
- THE SCALE FACTOR

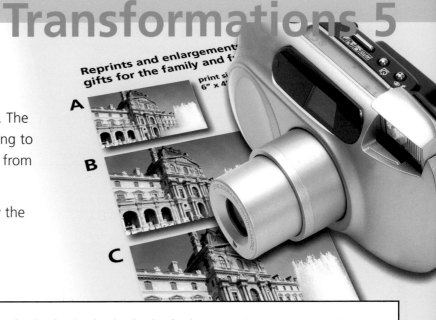

Scale Factor Greater Than 1

A Scale Factor greater than 1 means that the size of the image is bigger than the size of the object. Triangle A'B'C' is an enlargement of triangle ABC by a scale factor of 2, centre (0,0).

and
A'B' = 2 x AB   OA' = 2 x OA
A'C' = 2 x AC   OB' = 2 x OB
B'C' = 2 x BC   OC' = 2 x OC

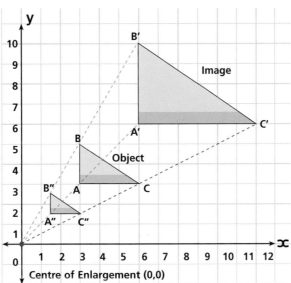

Centre of Enlargement (0,0)

Scale Factor Less Than 1

A Scale Factor less than 1 means that the size of the image is smaller than the size of the object. Triangle A"B"C" is an 'enlargement' of Triangle ABC by a scale factor of $\frac{1}{2}$, centre (0,0).

and
A"B" = $\frac{1}{2}$ x AB   OA" = $\frac{1}{2}$ x OA
A"C" = $\frac{1}{2}$ x AC   OB" = $\frac{1}{2}$ x OB
B"C" = $\frac{1}{2}$ x BC   OC" = $\frac{1}{2}$ x OC

Enlargement only changes the SIZE of the shape (i.e. the lengths of its sides) and its POSITION. Sometimes you are asked to calculate the Scale Factor and find the Centre of Enlargement.

The scale factor of any enlargement is equal to the ratio of the lengths of any two corresponding sides in the object and the image.

Example

Triangle P'Q'R' is an enlargement of triangle PQR. What is the Scale Factor of the enlargement and the coordinates of the Centre of Enlargement?

To find the Centre of Enlargement:
Draw dotted lines passing through P and P' (----), Q and Q' (——), R and R' (----) where these dotted lines cross is the Centre of Enlargement. Coordinates are (0, 1)

To find the Scale Factor of the enlargement:
P'Q' = 10 units, PQ = 2 units, P'Q' = 5 x PQ.
Scale Factor of the enlargement is 5

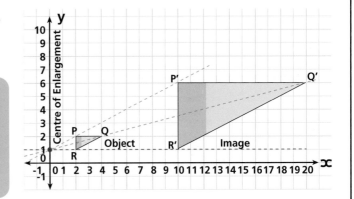

Transformations 6

Combination of Transformations

Very often a combination of two (or more) transformations
can be described by a single transformation.

Examples...

① Triangle ABC is reflected in the **y**-axis to A'B'C'
and then A'B'C' is reflected in the **x**-axis to
A"B"C". Draw the two transformations and
describe fully the single transformation that
maps triangle ABC onto triangle A"B"C".

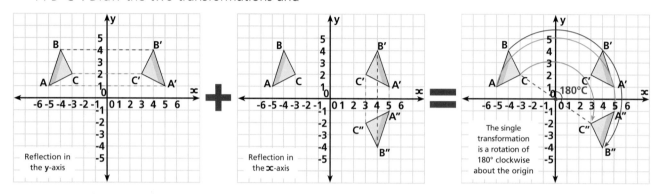

② Shape A is rotated 90° clockwise about the
origin to shape B. Shape B is then reflected
in the **x**-axis to shape C. Draw the two
transformations and describe fully the single
transformation that maps shape A onto shape C.

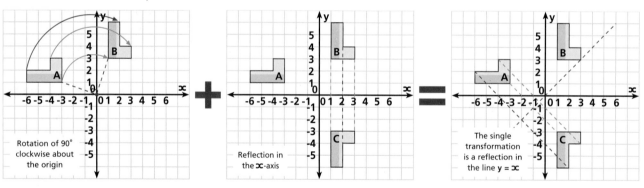

Characteristics of Transformations - A Summary

TRANSFORMATION / CHARACTERISTIC	You need to specify...	Properties that are preserved	Properties that change	Congruent or Similar?
REFLECTION	• The mirror line (equation of the line of reflection)	Shape and Size (e.g. angles, lengths of sides)	Orientation, Position	Congruent
ROTATION	• Direction of turn • Centre of Rotation • Angle turned through	As above	Orientation, Position	Congruent
TRANSLATION	• Direction of movement • Distance moved	As above plus orientation	Position	Congruent
ENLARGEMENT	• Centre of Enlargement • Scale Factor	Angles, ratios of lengths of side, orientation	Position, Size	Similar

Points on a Number Line

One coordinate is needed to identify a point on a number line, i.e. in 1-D (in one dimension). On this number line, point A is (-2) and point B is (3).

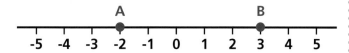

Points in a Plane

Two coordinates are needed to identify a point in a plane, i.e. in 2-D (in two dimensions). On the grid below point A is (3,4), B is (-2, 1) C is (-1, -4) and D is (1,-1).

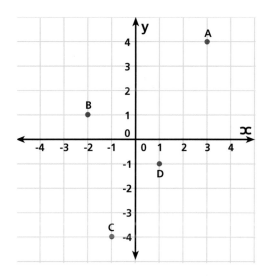

Coordinates can also be used to describe geometrical information. The coordinates of the following points: A is (3,2), B is (2, -2) C is (-3, -2) and D is (-2,2) are the vertices (corners) of a parallelogram.

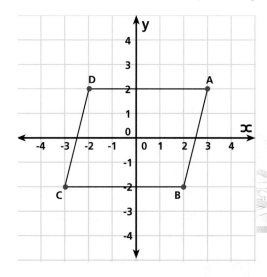

Points in Space

Three coordinates are needed to identify a point in space, i.e. in 3-D (in three dimensions). Three axes each at right angles to each other are needed. The coordinates of each point represent distances from **0**, a fixed point, firstly parallel to the **x**-axis then parallel to the **y**-axis, and finally parallel to the **z**-axis.

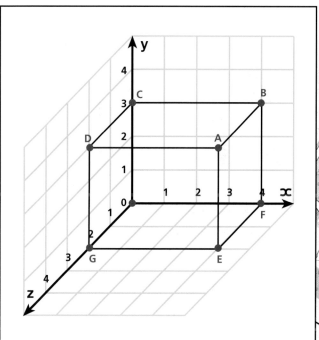

Point A is (4,3,2) since we need to go 4 units parallel to the **x**-axis, then 3 units parallel to the **y**-axis and finally 2 units parallel to the **z**-axis.

The other points would have the following coordinates: B is (4,3,0) C is (0,3,0) D is (0,3,2) E is (4,0,2) F is (4,0,0) and G is (0,0,2)

Picture courtesy of the AA

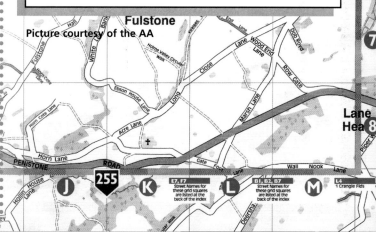

Coordinates 2

Coordinates of the Midpoint of a Line Segment

To find the coordinates of the midpoint, M, of a line segment AB you need to find…

- the average of the x coordinates of points A and B. This is the x coordinate of the midpoint, M.
- the average of the **y** coordinates of points A and B. This is the **y** coordinate of the midpoint, M.

Examples…

 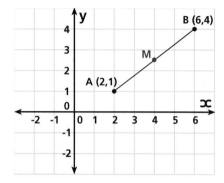

Average of x coordinates of points A and B

$$= \frac{2+6}{2} = \frac{8}{2} = 4$$

Average of **y** coordinates of points A and B

$$= \frac{1+4}{2} = \frac{5}{2} = 2.5$$

Coordinates of point M are (4,2.5)

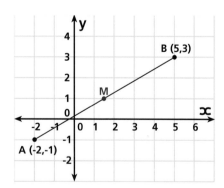

Average of x coordinates of points A and B

$$= \frac{-2+5}{2} = \frac{3}{2} = 1.5$$

Average of **y** coordinates of points A and B

$$= \frac{-1+3}{2} = \frac{2}{2} = 1$$

Coordinates of point M are (1.5,1)

Calculating the Length of a Line Segment

The length of a line segment AB can be found using Pythagoras' Theorem. Firstly complete the right-angled triangle ABC where AB represents the hypotenuse. You then find the length of AC and BC using the scale on the axes (not by using a ruler).

Examples…

 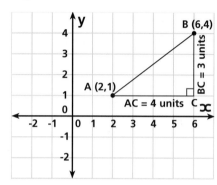

Using Pythagoras' Theorem

$$\mathbf{AB^2 = AC^2 + BC^2}$$
$$= 4^2 + 3^2$$
$$= 16 + 9$$
$$= 25$$
$$\mathbf{AB} = \sqrt{25}$$
$$= 5 \text{ units}$$

 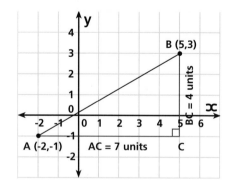

Using Pythagoras' Theorem

$$\mathbf{AB^2 = AC^2 + BC^2}$$
$$= 7^2 + 4^2$$
$$= 49 + 16$$
$$= 65$$
$$\mathbf{AB} = \sqrt{65} \text{ units (in surd form)}$$
$$= 8.1 \text{ units (to 2 sig. fig.)}$$

Perimeter

This is a measure of the distance all the way around the outside of a shape. All we need to know are the lengths of all the sides that make up the shape and then simply add them together.

Examples...

1

The lengths of all the sides are given or can be worked out and so...

Perimeter
= Length of AB + BC + CD + DE + EF + FA
= 6cm + 2.5cm + 4cm + (4.1 - 2.5)cm + 2cm + 4.1cm
= 20.2cm (remember the units)

2

The lengths of all the sides have to be measured using a ruler and so...

Perimeter
= Length of AB + BC + CA
= 6.2cm + 5.7cm + 4.3cm
= 16.2cm (remember the units)

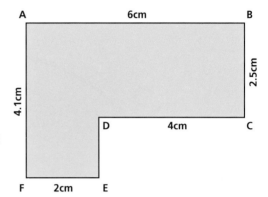

3

The lengths of all the sides can be found by counting squares and so...

Perimeter
= Length of AB + BC + CD + DE + EF + FA
= 1cm + 3cm + 1cm + 1cm + 2cm + 4cm
= 12cm (remember the units)

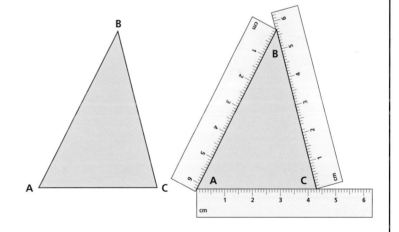

Perimeter 2

Circumference of a Circle

The circumference of a circle is a measure of the distance all the way around the outside of it. (Circumference is a mathematical word for the perimeter of a circle).

The **radius** is the distance from the centre, •, to the outside of the circle. The **diameter** is the distance from one side of the circle through the centre, •, to the other side of the circle which therefore means that:

> **Length of Radius = $\frac{1}{2}$ x Length of Diameter**
>
> or **Length of Diameter = 2 x Length of Radius**

The circumference can be found by using this formula:

> **Circumference = 2πr or Circumference = πd**

where π (called 'pi') has a value of 3.14 and 2πr means 2 x π x r and πd means π x d.

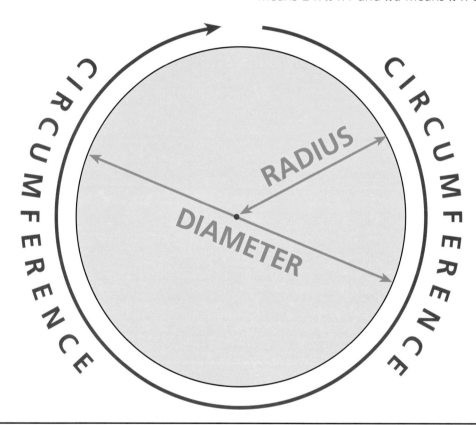

Examples...

1 A circle has a radius of 2cm. Calculate its circumference.

Using our formula:
C = 2πr

> We use this formula since we are given the RADIUS

C = 2 x π x 2cm
C = 2 x 3.14 x 2cm
C = 12.56cm (remember the units)

2 A corn circle has a diameter of 20m. Calculate its circumference.

Using our formula:
C = πd

> We use this formula since we are given the DIAMETER

C = π x 20m
C = 3.14 x 20m
C = 62.8m (remember the units)

Area

This is a measure of the amount of surface a two dimensional shape covers. Area is usually measured in **units²**, e.g. **cm²** (cm squared) or **m²** (m squared).

Estimation of Area Using Squared Paper

The area of a shape can be estimated if it has been drawn on squared paper. All we have to do is count the number of squares taken up by the shape.

This method is particularly useful when we have irregular shapes, although our answer will be an estimate of the area and not an exact value.

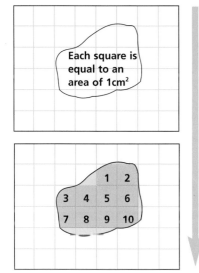

Each square is equal to an area of 1cm²

Count the whole squares and any squares more than half covered

Area = 10cm²

Areas of Common Shapes

The following shapes each have a formula which can be used to work out their area exactly.

Square

Rectangle

Parallelogram

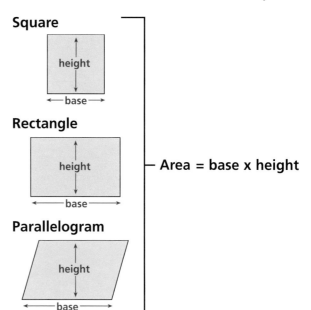

Area = base x height

Triangle

Area = $\frac{1}{2}$ x base x height

or ... = $\frac{\text{base x height}}{2}$

Trapezium

Area = $\frac{1}{2}$ (a + b) h

or ... = $\frac{(a + b)}{2}$ x h

Examples...

1 Calculate the area of the following trapezium.

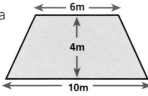

Using our formula: Area = $\frac{(a + b)}{2}$ x h

Area = $\frac{(10m + 6m)}{2}$ x 4m

= $\frac{16m}{2}$ x 4m

= 8m x 4m

= **32m²** (remember the units)

2 The following parallelogram has an area of 24cm². Calculate its height if the length of its base is 10cm.

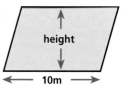

Using our formula: **Area = Base x Height**

24cm² = 10cm x Height

$\frac{24}{10}$ = $\frac{\cancel{10}}{\cancel{10}}$ x Height

Divide both sides by 10 to give us height on its own

Height = 2.4cm (remember the units)

Area 2

Deducing the Formula for the Area of a Parallelogram

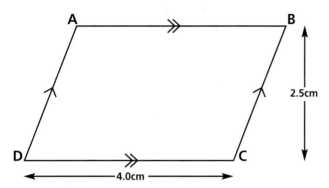

The base of the parallelogram above is 4cm long and the perpendicular height is 2.5cm.

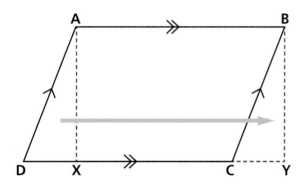

If we cut the triangle **ADX** off one side of the parallelogram and move it to the other side to form **BCY**, we create rectangle **ABYX**...

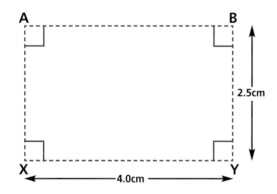

... which has exactly the same area as our original parallelogram. Since...

Area of a Rectangle = Base x Height
= 4 x 2.5
= 10.0cm²

... this must also be the area of the parallelogram.

Area of a Parallelogram = Base x Height

Deducing the Formula for the Area of a Triangle

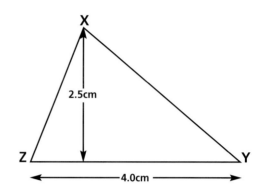

The base of the triangle above is 4cm long and the perpendicular height is 2.5cm.

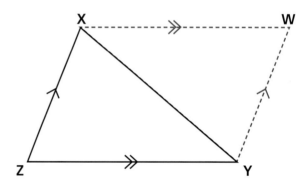

By drawing in the lines **XW** and **WY** we create a parallelogram. However the triangles **XYZ** and **XYW** are congruent (the same size and shape)...

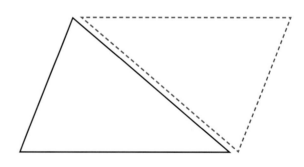

... which means that they have equal areas and are therefore exactly half of the area of the parallelogram.

Since the area of a parallelogram is equal to the base multiplied by the height, it follows that...

Area of a Triangle = $\frac{1}{2}$ Base x Height

= $\frac{1}{2}$ (4 x 2.5)

= 5.0cm²

Area of a Circle

The area of a circle is given by the formula:

$$\text{Area} = \pi r^2$$

Radius

Yet again π has a value of **3.14** and πr^2 means π **x radius squared** or π **x r x r**. Don't get too worried about π (pi), it's just a different way of saying **3.14**…

Example…

A circular cricket field has a radius of 80m. Calculate its area ($\pi = 3.14$).

Using our formula:

$$\begin{aligned}\text{Area} &= \pi r^2 \\ &= 3.14 \times 80^2 \\ &= 3.14 \times 6\,400 \\ &= 20\,096\text{m}^2\end{aligned}$$

Areas of Compound Shapes

These are shapes that can be divided up into smaller shapes. The area of each of these smaller shapes can then be calculated and added together.

Example…

The diagram shows the layout for a side wall of a house. Calculate its area.

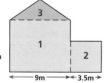

Area of 1 (Rectangle) = 9m x 8m = 72m^2
Area of 2 (Square) = 3.5m x 3.5m = 12.25m^2

Area of 3 (Triangle) = $\dfrac{9\text{m} \times 4\text{m}}{2}$ = 18m^2

$$\begin{aligned}\textbf{Area of wall} &= \textbf{Area 1 + Area 2 + Area 3} \\ &= \textbf{72m}^2 + \textbf{12.25m}^2 + \textbf{18m}^2 \\ &= \textbf{102.25m}^2 \text{ (remember the units)}\end{aligned}$$

Surface Area of Solids

The surface area of any solid is simply the area of the NET which can be folded to completely cover the outside of the solid.

Examples…

1 Calculate the surface area of the following triangular prism which has an equilateral triangle as its cross-section.

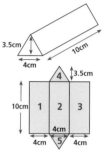

Area of 1 (Rectangle) = 10cm x 4cm = 40cm^2
Therefore Area of 2 + 3 = 80cm^2

Area of 4 (Triangle) = $\dfrac{4\text{cm} \times 3.5\text{cm}}{2}$ = 7cm^2

Therefore Area of 5 = 7cm^2

$$\begin{aligned}\textbf{Surface Area of prism} & \\ &= \textbf{Area of 1 + 2 + 3 + 4 + 5} \\ &= \textbf{40cm}^2 + \textbf{80cm}^2 + \textbf{7cm}^2 + \textbf{7cm}^2 \\ &= \textbf{134cm}^2 \text{ (remember the units)}\end{aligned}$$

2 Calculate the surface area of this cylinder.

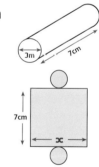

$$\begin{aligned}\textbf{Area of each end} &= \pi r^2 \\ &= \textbf{3.14} \times \textbf{1.5}^2 \\ &= \textbf{7.065cm}^2\end{aligned}$$

$$\begin{aligned}\textbf{Therefore both ends} & \\ &= \textbf{7.065} \times \textbf{2} = \textbf{14.13cm}^2\end{aligned}$$

$$\begin{aligned}\textbf{Length of } x &= \textbf{circumference of circle} \\ &= 2\pi r \\ &= \textbf{2} \times \textbf{3.14} \times \textbf{1.5} \\ &= \textbf{9.42cm}\end{aligned}$$

$$\begin{aligned}\textbf{Therefore area of rectangle} & \\ &= \textbf{7} \times \textbf{9.42} \\ &= \textbf{65.94cm}^2\end{aligned}$$

$$\begin{aligned}\textbf{Therefore total area} & \\ &= \textbf{14.13cm}^2 + \textbf{65.94cm}^2 \\ &= \textbf{80.07cm}^2\end{aligned}$$

Volume 1

Volume

This is a measure of the amount of space a 3-D object takes up. Volume is usually measured in **units³**, e.g. **cm³** (cm cubed) or **m³** (m cubed).

Calculation of the Volume of a Solid Made Up of Cubes

Providing we know the volume of one cube then all we have to do is work out how many cubes there are in each layer of the solid and then add them up.

Example

In the following example each cube 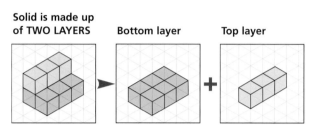 has a volume of 1cm³.

Solid is made up of TWO LAYERS   **Bottom layer**   **Top layer**

Volume = 6 cubes + 3 cubes = 6cm³ + 3cm³ = 9cm³

Volume of a Cuboid

The volume of a cuboid is given by the formula:

Volume = length x width x height
V = ℓ x w x h

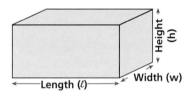

Example

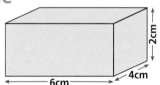

Using our formula:
Volume = length x width x height
    = 6cm x 4cm x 2cm
    = **48cm³** (remember the units)

Volume of a Prism

A prism is a solid which has a uniform cross-section from one end of the solid to the other end. The volume of any prism is given by the formula:

Volume of a prism
= area of cross-section x length

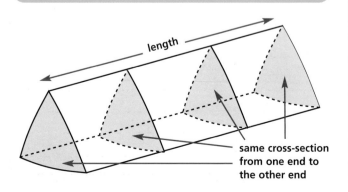

length

same cross-section from one end to the other end

Example

Calculate the volume of the following triangular prism.

The cross-section is obviously a TRIANGLE

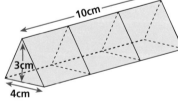

Using our formula:
Volume = area of cross-section x length

$$= \frac{(\text{base x height})}{2} \times \text{length}$$

$$= \frac{(4\text{cm x } 3\text{cm})}{2} \times 10\text{cm}$$

$$= 6\text{cm}^2 \times 10\text{cm} = 60\text{cm}^3$$

(remember the units)

Volume of a Cylinder

A cylinder is a prism which has a uniform cross-section of a circle from one end of the prism to the other. The volume of any cylinder is given by the formula:

> **Volume of a cylinder** $= \pi r^2 \ell = \pi r^2 \times \ell$
> (where ℓ is the length of the cylinder)

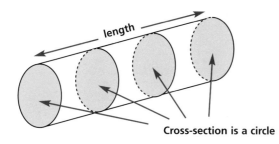

length

Cross-section is a circle

Examples...

1 Calculate the volume of the following cylinder (let $\pi = 3.14$)

8cm

2cm

Using our formula:
Volume $= \pi r^2 \ell$
Volume $= \pi r^2 \times$ **length**

$\quad = 3.14 \times (2cm)^2 \times 8cm$
$\quad = 3.14 \times 4cm^2 \times 8cm$
$\quad = \mathbf{100.48\ cm^3}$ (remember the units)

2 A cylindrical tank is 1.6m long and holds $0.8m^3$ of oil when full. What is the radius of the cylinder (let $\pi = 3.14$).

1.6m

Using our formula:
Volume $= \pi r^2 \ell$
$0.8m^3 = 3.14 \times r^2 \times 1.6m$
$0.8m^3 = 5.024m \times r^2$

$\dfrac{0.8m^3}{5.024m} = \dfrac{5.024m}{5.024m} \times r^2$

> Divide both sides by 5.024 to leave r^2 on its own

$0.159m^2 = r^2$
$\sqrt{0.159m^2} = \sqrt{r^2}$

> Take square root of both sides to leave r on its own

$r = \mathbf{0.40m}$ (to 2 d.p.)
(remember the units)

Distinguishing between Formulae for Perimeter, Area and Volume

Any formula or expression for...

Perimeter - has only a single dimension 'length' in it, since its units are cm or m.

Area - has the dimensions of 'length x length' or 'length^2' in it, since its units are cm^2 or m^2.

Volume - has the dimensions of 'length x length x length' or 'length^3' in it, since its units are cm^3 or m^3.

All numbers and symbols (e.g. π) have no dimensions and therefore don't contribute to the units.

Important Point!

In your exam you may well be asked to distinguish between expressions representing length or perimeter, area, volume. These questions may take the following form:

Examples...

1 In the expressions in the table below, **a**, **b**, **c** and **d** represent lengths. All numbers and symbols have no dimensions. Tick the boxes beneath the expressions which could represent areas.

$\dfrac{\pi dcb}{2a}$	$\dfrac{a^3}{2}$	$4a^2$	$a^3 + b$	$\dfrac{a+b}{c}$	$3a^2 + b^2$	$3a^2b^2$
✓		✓			✓	

2 In the expressions in the table below, **p**, **q** and **r** represent lengths. Tick the appropriate box to indicate whether the expression represents a length, an area, a volume or none of these.

Expression	Length	Area	Volume	None
pq + qr		✓		
p x q x r			✓	
p + q + r	✓			
p^{2}qr				✓

3-D Shapes 1

Solids

A solid is a three-dimensional (3-D) shape. A very simple solid is the CUBE (a box with all its sides equal in length).

Here are some more examples of some common solids:

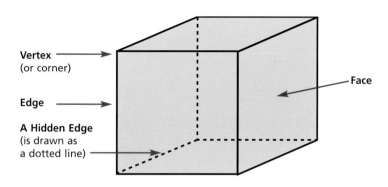

Vertex (or corner)

Edge

A Hidden Edge (is drawn as a dotted line)

Face

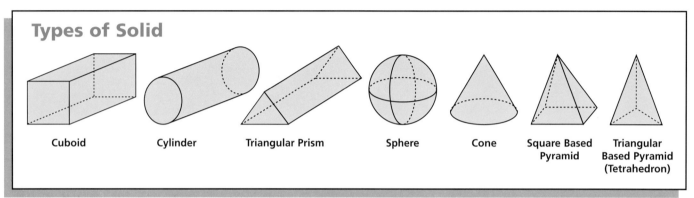

Types of Solid

Cuboid   Cylinder   Triangular Prism   Sphere   Cone   Square Based Pyramid   Triangular Based Pyramid (Tetrahedron)

Drawing Solids Using Isometric Paper

A disadvantage of drawing solids like the ones above is that accurate measurements of all sides cannot be taken from the diagram. One way of drawing solids is to use isometric paper. This is a grid of equilateral triangles or dots. All solids can be drawn accurately and all measurements can be taken from the diagram.

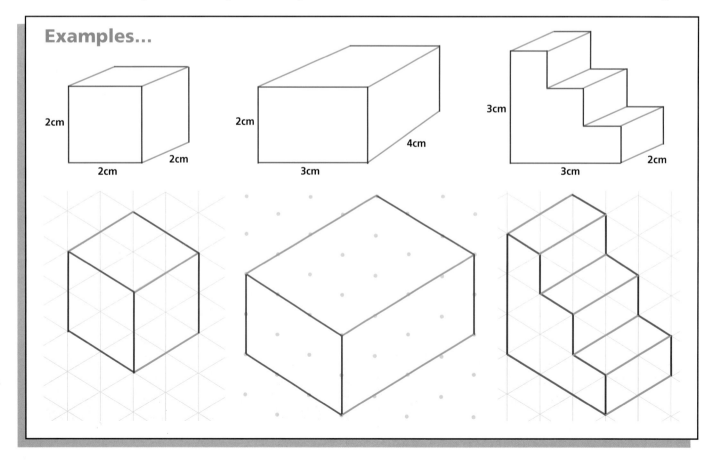

Examples...

2cm 2cm 2cm

2cm 3cm 4cm

3cm 3cm 2cm

Plans and Elevations

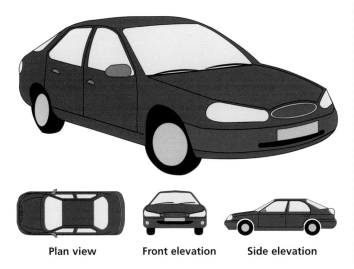

Plan view   Front elevation   Side elevation

This is a picture of a car (a three-dimensional view of a solid). It is possible for us to have THREE different views of the car

- PLAN VIEW where we look down on the car from above
- FRONT ELEVATION where we look at the car from the front
- SIDE ELEVATION where we look at the car from the side

Example

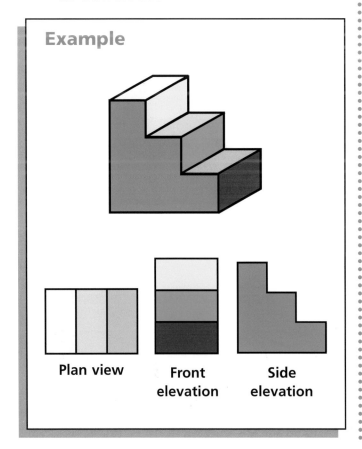

Plan view   Front elevation   Side elevation

Nets for Solids

A net is a two-dimensional shape which can be folded to completely cover the outside of a solid.

Example

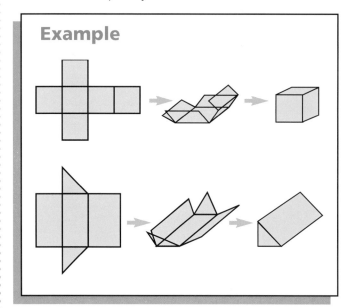

Plane Symmetry

A solid has plane symmetry if it can be 'cut in half' so that one half of the solid is an exact mirror image of the other half.

Examples...

A cuboid has three planes of symmetry

A square based pyramid has four planes of symmetry

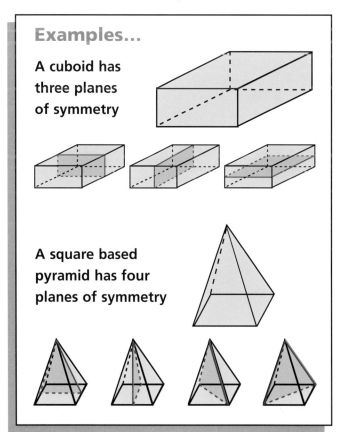

Symmetry 1

Line or Reflective Symmetry

A two-dimensional shape has a LINE OF SYMMETRY if it can be 'cut in half' so that one half of the shape is an exact mirror image of the other half of the shape.

The shapes opposite have 1 line of symmetry. These shapes can be 'cut in half' only once, and one half of the shape is congruent to the other half.

It is also possible for shapes to have more than 1 line of symmetry. The shapes below can be 'cut in half' more than once.

A simple way to find lines of symmetry is to use tracing paper.

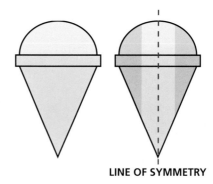

LINE OF SYMMETRY

The left hand side of the dotted line is an exact mirror image of the right hand side and vice-versa

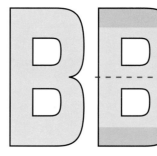

LINE OF SYMMETRY

The top side of the dotted line is an exact mirror image of the bottom side and vice-versa

---

Two Lines of Symmetry

Draw in where you think the line of symmetry is and trace one side of your shape carefully on the tracing paper.

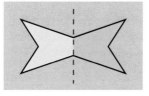 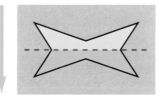

Flip the tracing paper over about the line of symmetry. If your line of symmetry is correct you should get an exact mirror image.

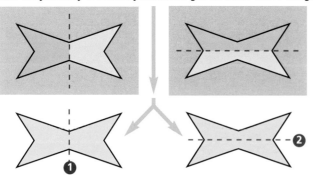

Three Lines of Symmetry

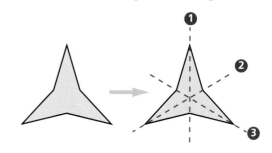

Four Lines of Symmetry

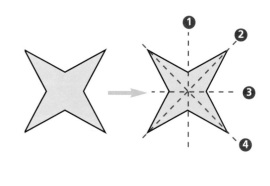

Some shapes, especially regular polygons (see p.64) can have even more lines of symmetry and there are shapes that have NO LINES OF SYMMETRY. These shapes cannot be 'cut in half' to give exact mirror images. Use tracing paper to check that the following shapes have no lines of symmetry.

Lonsdale

Rotational Symmetry

A two-dimensional shape has ROTATIONAL SYMMETRY if it can be 'rotated about a point', called the Centre of Rotation, to a different position so that it looks the same as it was to begin with. The Order of Rotational Symmetry is equal to the number of times a shape fits onto itself in one 360° turn.

The following shape has ROTATIONAL SYMMETRY ORDER 2. This shape looks the same as its original position every time it is rotated half a turn (180°).

Rotational Symmetry Order 2

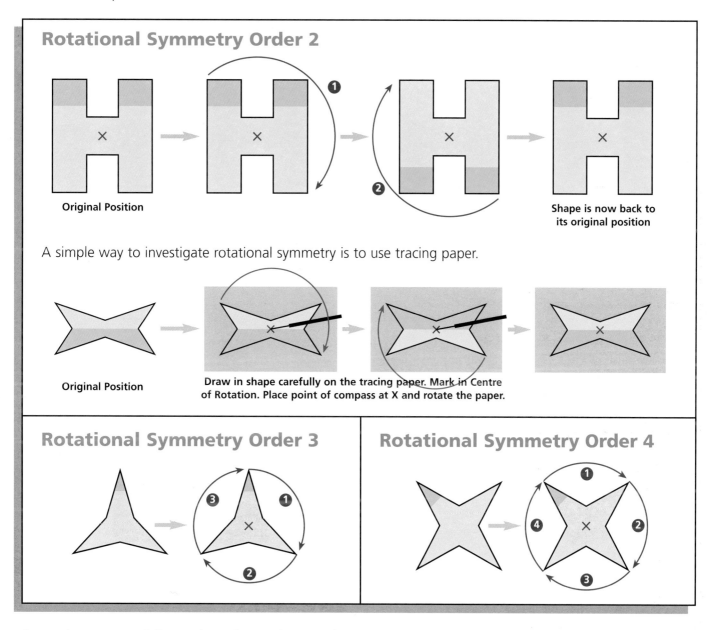

Original Position

Shape is now back to its original position

A simple way to investigate rotational symmetry is to use tracing paper.

Original Position

Draw in shape carefully on the tracing paper. Mark in Centre of Rotation. Place point of compass at X and rotate the paper.

Rotational Symmetry Order 3

Rotational Symmetry Order 4

Some shapes, especially regular polygons (see p.64) can have rotational symmetry of even higher orders and there are shapes that have ROTATIONAL SYMMETRY ORDER 1 (this can also be referred to as NO ROTATIONAL SYMMETRY). These shapes only look the same as their original position when they have been rotated one complete turn (360°)!!

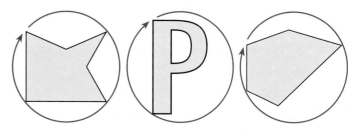

Scale Drawings and Map Scales

Drawing to Size and Scale

Before you attempt to construct any drawing to a particular size or scale you need the following:

- A PENCIL so any mistakes can be rubbed out without making a mess (and it looks a lot neater anyway).

- A RULER for the drawing of all straight lines.
- A PROTRACTOR for the measuring of any angles.
- A COMPASS for drawing circles, arcs and for any constructions.

Example

Here is a sketch map of an island. The map has four marker points A, B, C and D.

a) Make an accurate scale drawing of the quadrilateral ABCD using a scale of 1cm to represent 10km.

b) Calculate the length of BC.

a) **Step 1: Draw the 90km line (9cm = 90km).**
   Step 2: Measure and mark 80° and 90°.
   Step 3: Draw the 35km line (3.5cm = 35km) and the 45km line (4.5cm = 45km).
   Step 4: Complete the quadrilateral.

b) **Length of BC = 8.4cm = 8.4 x 10km = 84km**

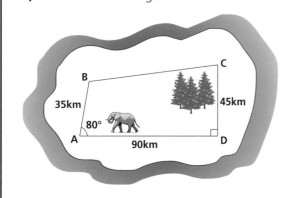

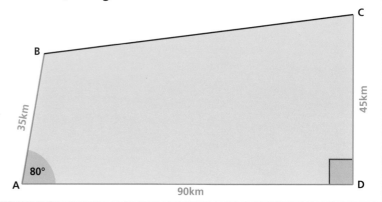

Map Scales

This is part of a map of Devon and Cornwall which is drawn to a scale of 1cm : 10km

1. The direct distance from Newquay to Plymouth as measured on the map is 7cm. Calculate the actual distance.

   Actual dist = Map dist x 10

   = 7 x 10 = 70km

2. The actual direct distance between Torquay and Exeter is 30km. Calculate the map distance.

   Map dist = Actual dist ÷ 10

   $= \frac{30}{10} = 3cm$

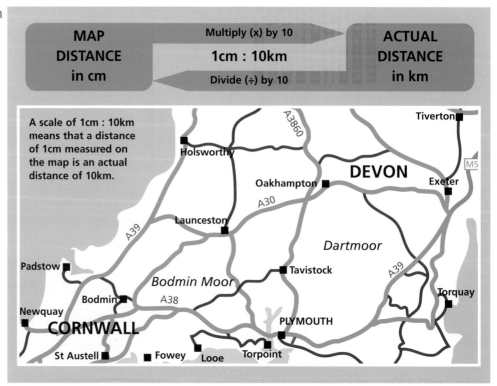

A scale of 1cm : 10km means that a distance of 1cm measured on the map is an actual distance of 10km.

Measuring Bearings

Three-Figure Bearings

A bearing is a measurement of the position of one point relative to another point. It is measured in degrees. **Bearings are always measured from the north in a clockwise direction and are given as 3 digits**. Below are two points, A and B. There are TWO possible bearings:

- The bearing of B from point A. This means that the measurement of the bearing is taken from point A.
- The bearing of A from point B. This means that the measurement of the bearing is taken from point B.

A circular protractor with a full 360° range can make three-figure bearings much easier to measure.

Sometimes the angle you measure from the N direction is less than 100° or even less than 10°. In this case one or two zeros are put in front of the angle in order to make them THREE-FIGURE BEARINGS.

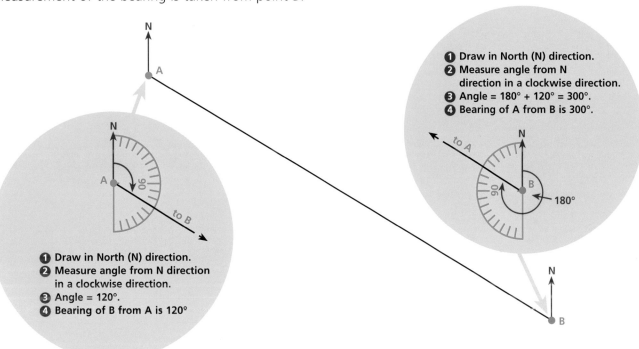

❶ Draw in North (N) direction.
❷ Measure angle from N direction in a clockwise direction.
❸ Angle = 120°.
❹ Bearing of B from A is 120°

❶ Draw in North (N) direction.
❷ Measure angle from N direction in a clockwise direction.
❸ Angle = 180° + 120° = 300°.
❹ Bearing of A from B is 300°.

Examples...

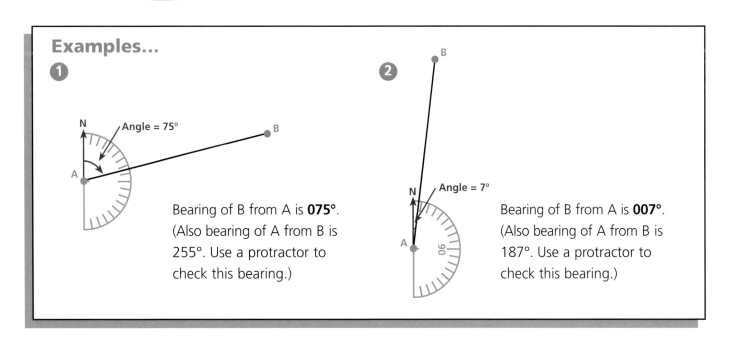

❶ Bearing of B from A is **075°**. (Also bearing of A from B is 255°. Use a protractor to check this bearing.)

❷ Bearing of B from A is **007°**. (Also bearing of A from B is 187°. Use a protractor to check this bearing.)

Reading Scales

Count Patterns

Most scales use simple count patterns based on the two, four, five or ten 'times' tables. They rely on the basic rules of decimals and fractions.

Once you have identified the count pattern you can take a reading on any straight, curved, horizontal or vertical scale.

Look at the different count patterns on these scales:

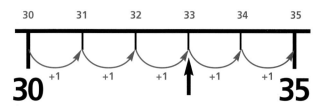

This scale goes up by one each time. In other words it has a count pattern of +1. So, the arrow gives a reading of 33.

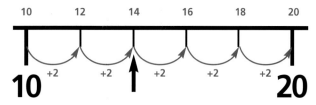

This scale goes up by two each time. In other words it has a count pattern of +2. The arrow gives a reading of 14.

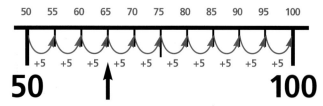

This scale goes up by five each time. In other words it has a count pattern of +5. The arrow gives a reading of 65.

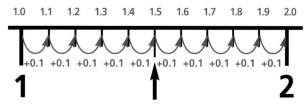

This scale goes up by 0.1 (or $\frac{1}{10}$) each time. In other words it has a count pattern of +0.1. The arrow gives a reading of 1.5.

Examples...

1 What is the reading on the thermometer?

> - First you need to identify the count pattern. The numbers on the scale increase in tens. The lines in between have a count pattern of +1.
> - Then you can take an accurate reading by counting up the scale from 20 (the last marked number) in ones.

20 + 4 = 24°

2 How much fruit juice has been collected in this measuring jug?

> - Identify the count pattern. This time the numbers on the scale increase in fifties. The lines in between have a count pattern of +5.
> - Take an accurate reading by counting up the scale from 50 (the last marked number) in fives.

50 + 45 = 95ml

3 A car tyre needs a pressure of 34psi. The pressure gauge shows the current pressure. How many more psi are needed in the tyre?

> - Identify the count pattern. Again, the numbers on the scale increase in tens, but this time the lines in between have a count pattern of +2.
> - Take an accurate reading by counting up the scale from 20 (the last marked number) in twos: 20 + 2 = 22psi.
> - Now you can calculate the answer.

34 - 22 = 12psi needed.

You can check your answer by counting up the scale from 22 to 34.

Converting Measurements

Metric and Imperial Units

	Metric units	Approximate comparison between Metric & Imperial	Imperial units
Length	10mm = 1cm 100cm = 1m 1000m = 1km	2.5cm ≈ 1 inch 1m ≈ 39 inches 1600m ≈ 1 mile 8km ≈ 5 miles	12 inches = 1 foot 3 feet = 1 yard 1760 yards = 1 mile
Mass	1000mg = 1g 1000g = 1kg 1000kg = 1 tonne	30g ≈ 1 ounce 450g ≈ 1 pound 1kg ≈ 2.2 pounds	16 ounces = 1 pound 14 pounds = 1 stone
Capacity or Volume	1000ml = 1l 1000cm³ = 1l (1ml = 1cm³)	1l ≈ $1\frac{3}{4}$ pints 4.5l ≈ 1 gallon	8 pints = 1 gallon

Converting One Metric Unit to Another

Consider the conversion between centimetres (cm) and metres (m) as a typical example:

Divide (÷) by 100 as we are going from a bigger number (100) to a smaller number (1)

100cm   100cm = 1m   **1m**

Multiply (x) by 100 as we are going from a smaller number (1) to a bigger number (100)

Examples...

1 Convert 300cm to metres.

From above: cm $\xrightarrow{\div\,100}$ m

$300\text{cm} = \dfrac{300}{100} = 3\text{m}$

2 Penny is 1.65m tall. What is her height in centimetres?

From above: m $\xrightarrow{\times\,100}$ cm

$1.65\text{m} = 1.65 \times 100 = 165\text{cm}$

Converting Between Metric and Imperial Units

These follow the same rules. Take the conversion between grams (g) and pounds.

Divide (÷) by 450

450g   450g ≈ 1 pound   **1 pound**

Multiply (x) by 450

Examples...

1 A tin of baked beans has a mass of 600g. What is its mass in pounds?

From above: g $\xrightarrow{\div\,450}$ pounds

$600\text{g} = \dfrac{600}{450} = 1.33$ **pounds** (approx.)

2 A recipe for a cake needs 1.5 pounds of flour. What mass of flour is needed in grams?

From above: pounds $\xrightarrow{\times\,450}$ g

1.5 **pounds** $= 1.5 \times 450 = 675\text{g}$ (approx.)

Compound Measures

Speed

This is a measure of how fast an object is moving. To calculate the speed of a moving object we need two measurements:

- the **DISTANCE** it moves and
- the **TIME** it takes to move that distance.

Speed can be calculated using the formula…

$$\text{Speed (S)} = \frac{\text{Distance (D)}}{\text{Time (T)}}$$

Speed is measured - in metres per second, m/s
- or kilometres per hour, km/h
- or miles per hour, mph

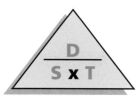 A FORMULA TRIANGLE makes it a lot easier for us when we want to calculate distance or time.

 To get the formula for DISTANCE, cover 'D' up

DISTANCE = SPEED x TIME

 To get the formula for TIME, cover 'T' up

$$\textbf{TIME} = \frac{\textbf{DISTANCE}}{\textbf{SPEED}}$$

Examples...

1 Calculate the speed of a car which travels a distance of 90m in 10s.

$$\textbf{Speed} = \frac{\textbf{90m}}{\textbf{10}} = \textbf{9m/s} \text{ (remember the units)}$$

2 A train completes a journey of 150km at an average speed of 90km/h. How long did the journey take?

$$\textbf{Time} = \frac{\textbf{Distance}}{\textbf{Speed}} = \frac{\textbf{150km}}{\textbf{90km/h}}$$

$$= \textbf{1.}\dot{\textbf{6}} = \textbf{1}\tfrac{\textbf{2}}{\textbf{3}} = \textbf{1 hour 40 minutes}$$
(remember the units)

Density

This is a measure of how heavy an object is per unit volume. To calculate the density of an object we need two measurements:

- its **MASS** and
- its **VOLUME**.

Density can be calculated using the formula…

$$\text{Density (D)} = \frac{\text{Mass (M)}}{\text{Volume (V)}}$$

Density is measured
- in grams per centimetre cubed, g/cm^3
- or kilograms per metre cubed, kg/m^3

 A FORMULA TRIANGLE makes it a lot easier for us when we want to calculate mass or volume.

 To get the formula for MASS, cover 'M' up

MASS = DENSITY x VOLUME

 To get the formula for VOLUME, cover 'V' up

$$\textbf{VOLUME} = \frac{\textbf{MASS}}{\textbf{DENSITY}}$$

Example...

Calculate the density of an object which has a mass of 75g and a volume of $100cm^3$.

$$\textbf{Density} = \frac{\textbf{75g}}{\textbf{100cm}^3} = \textbf{0.75g/cm}^3 \text{ (remember the units)}$$

Construction of Triangles

If you are given...

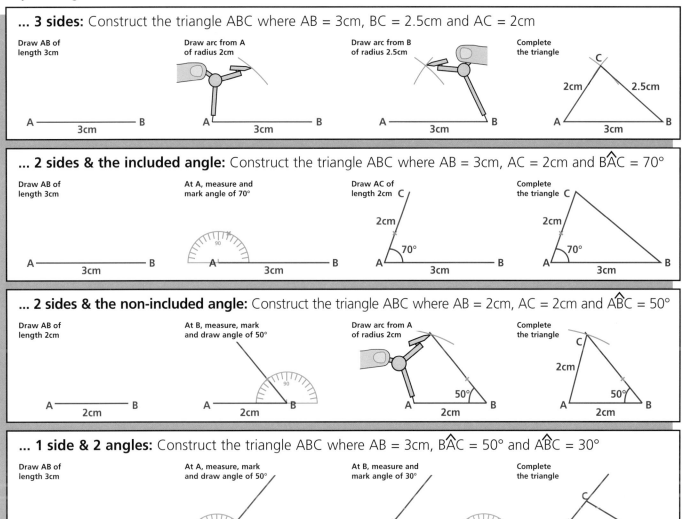

... 3 sides: Construct the triangle ABC where AB = 3cm, BC = 2.5cm and AC = 2cm

Draw AB of length 3cm

Draw arc from A of radius 2cm

Draw arc from B of radius 2.5cm

Complete the triangle

... 2 sides & the included angle: Construct the triangle ABC where AB = 3cm, AC = 2cm and BÂC = 70°

Draw AB of length 3cm

At A, measure and mark angle of 70°

Draw AC of length 2cm

Complete the triangle

... 2 sides & the non-included angle: Construct the triangle ABC where AB = 2cm, AC = 2cm and AB̂C = 50°

Draw AB of length 2cm

At B, measure, mark and draw angle of 50°

Draw arc from A of radius 2cm

Complete the triangle

... 1 side & 2 angles: Construct the triangle ABC where AB = 3cm, BÂC = 50° and AB̂C = 30°

Draw AB of length 3cm

At A, measure, mark and draw angle of 50°

At B, measure and mark angle of 30°

Complete the triangle

Construction of an Angle of 60° and 90°

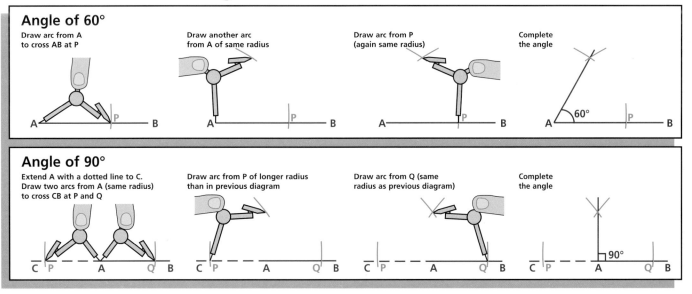

Angle of 60°

Draw arc from A to cross AB at P

Draw another arc from A of same radius

Draw arc from P (again same radius)

Complete the angle

Angle of 90°

Extend A with a dotted line to C. Draw two arcs from A (same radius) to cross CB at P and Q

Draw arc from P of longer radius than in previous diagram

Draw arc from Q (same radius as previous diagram)

Complete the angle

Constructions 2

The Midpoint and Perpendicular Bisector of a Line Segment

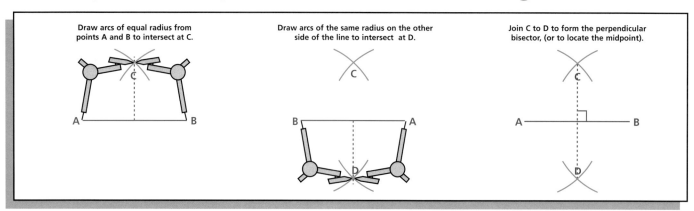

Draw arcs of equal radius from points A and B to intersect at C.

Draw arcs of the same radius on the other side of the line to intersect at D.

Join C to D to form the perpendicular bisector, (or to locate the midpoint).

The Perpendicular from a Point to a Line

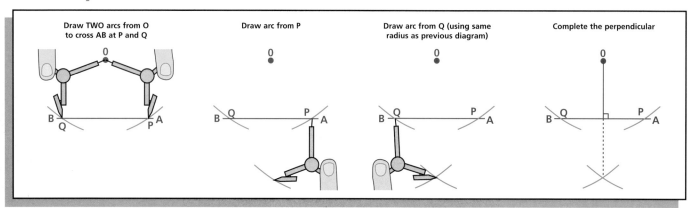

Draw TWO arcs from O to cross AB at P and Q

Draw arc from P

Draw arc from Q (using same radius as previous diagram)

Complete the perpendicular

The Perpendicular from a Point on a Line

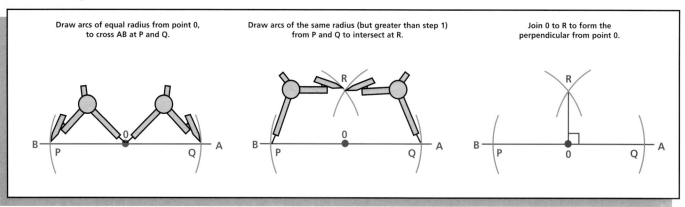

Draw arcs of equal radius from point 0, to cross AB at P and Q.

Draw arcs of the same radius (but greater than step 1) from P and Q to intersect at R.

Join 0 to R to form the perpendicular from point 0.

The Bisector of an Angle

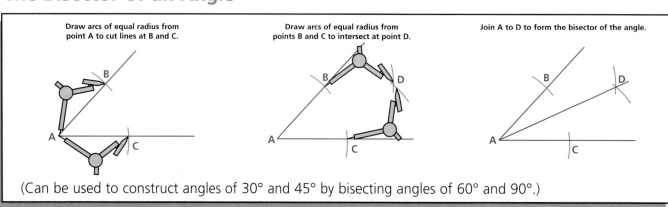

Draw arcs of equal radius from point A to cut lines at B and C.

Draw arcs of equal radius from points B and C to intersect at point D.

Join A to D to form the bisector of the angle.

(Can be used to construct angles of 30° and 45° by bisecting angles of 60° and 90°.)

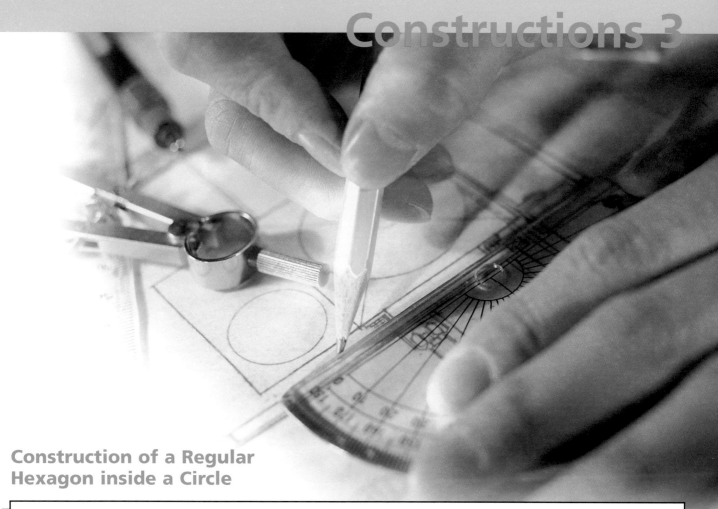

Construction of a Regular Hexagon inside a Circle

A simple way to do this is as follows:

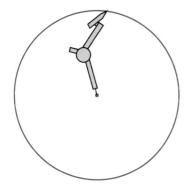

First of all construct the circle with the radius you require.

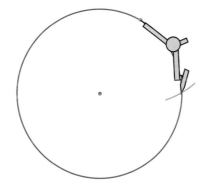

Using the same radius, place the compass point anywhere on the circumference and draw an arc.

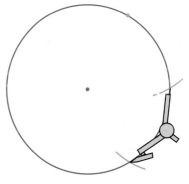

Using the same radius again, place the compass on the point where the arc intersects the circumference and draw another arc.

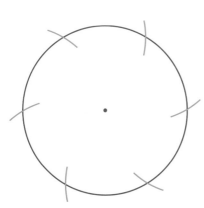

Repeat this process until you have six equal arcs on the circumference of the circle. The final arc should intersect the circumference at your starting point.

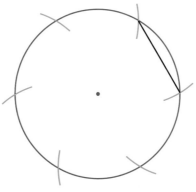

Use a ruler to draw a straight line between the first two points where the arcs intersect the circumference of the circle.

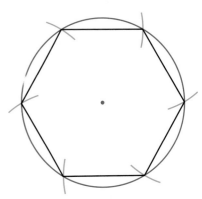

Repeat this process, joining up all the points to form a regular hexagon.

Loci

A locus is a line, all the points of which follow a particular rule. You need to know the following loci. The rule of each locus is in the box alongside the diagrams.

The locus of points which are always at a constant distance from a point … is a CIRCLE whose radius is equal to the constant distance.	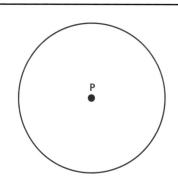
The locus of points which are always at a constant distance from a line… is a PAIR OF PARALLEL LINES, one above and one below the line with a PAIR OF SEMI-CIRCLES, one at each end of the line.	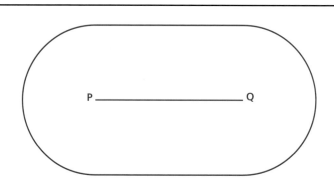
The locus of points which are always equidistant from two points… is a LINE WHICH BISECTS THE TWO POINTS AT RIGHT ANGLES (i.e. a perpendicular bisector). P ●--------□--------● Q	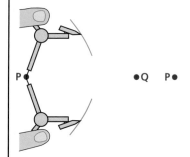 Draw TWO arcs from P Draw TWO arcs from Q (same radius as from P) 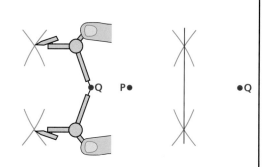 Draw the line from one intersection of arcs to the other.
The locus of points which are always equidistant from two lines… is a LINE WHICH BISECTS THE ANGLE BETWEEN THE TWO LINES (i.e. an angle bisector). 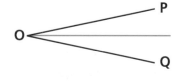	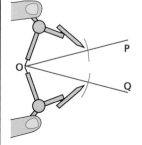 Draw TWO arcs from O to cross the lines OP and OQ Draw TWO arcs from where the first two arcs cross the lines to form point R. 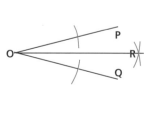 Draw the line from R to O to form the angle bisector.

Properties of Circles

The following nine diagrams relate to terms used to describe various properties of circles. You need to be completely familiar with all of these.

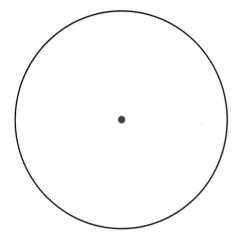

The CENTRE of the circle is the only point which is the same distance from every point on the circumference.

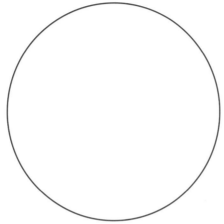

The CIRCUMFERENCE is the line which defines the edge of the circle. It is always the same distance from the centre of the circle.

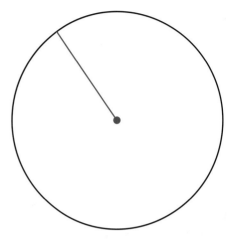

The RADIUS is formed by any straight line drawn from the centre of the circle to the circumference. It is always half the diameter of the circle.

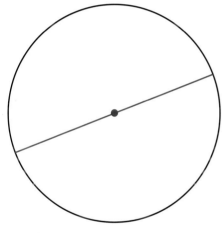

The DIAMETER is a straight line which passes through the centre of the circle to join opposite points on the circumference.

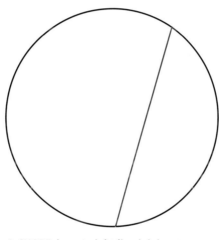

A CHORD is a straight line joining two points on the circumference which DOES NOT pass through the centre of the circle.

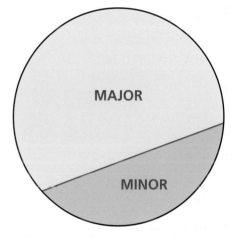

SEGMENTS are formed by a chord. The larger segment is called the major segment and the smaller one is called the minor segment.

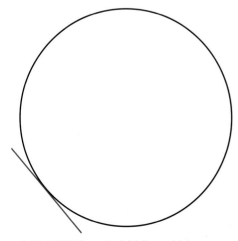

A TANGENT is a straight line which touches the circumference of a circle.

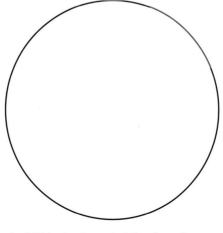

An ARC is simply part of the circumference of a circle.

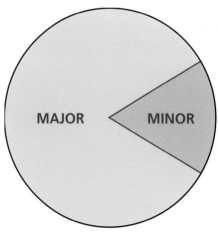

A SECTOR is the area enclosed by two radii and an arc. It can be major or minor.

Probability

The Nature of Probability

Probability, quite simply is a measure of the likelihood of a particular event occurring. Probability is used throughout the world in order to give a sound mathematical basis for predicting future events. These events can be relatively simple such as tossing a coin or spinning a roulette wheel, however they can also be vastly complicated such as in the assessment of a large insurance risk.

Probability Scale and the Language of Probability

For an event to happen we might say that its probability is 'a certainty', 'more than likely', 'evens' or '50/50', 'not very likely', 'no chance'. The probability of an event occurring (or not occurring) can be stated as either a fraction, percentage or decimal. These can be shown on a probability scale. Here is a very simple one:

These are the only probabilities you can have, i.e. you cannot have a probability greater than 1.
So, if the probability of something happening is P, then the probability of it not happening is 1 - P

0	$\frac{1}{10}$	$\frac{2}{10}$	$\frac{3}{10}$	$\frac{4}{10}$	$\frac{5}{10}$	$\frac{6}{10}$	$\frac{7}{10}$	$\frac{8}{10}$	$\frac{9}{10}$	1
0	10%	20%	30%	40%	50%	60%	70%	80%	90%	100%
0	0.1	0.2	0.3	0.4	0.5	0.6	0.7	0.8	0.9	1

No chance i.e. impossible	Not very likely	Evens 50/50	More than likely	A certainty i.e. bound to happen

Examples...

1 The probability of you passing a maths test is $\frac{7}{10}$. What is the probability that you will fail?

> Since you can only pass or fail, the total probability = 1. Therefore...

P(passing) + P(failing) = 1

P(failing) = 1 - P(passing)

$= 1 - \frac{7}{10}$

$= \frac{3}{10}$

> ... which means that you are not very likely to fail!

2 A drawer contains white, black and red socks only. If the probability of picking a white sock at random is 0.2 and a black sock is 0.3, what is the probability of picking a red sock?

> Since the drawer only contains white, black and red socks, the total probability = 1. Therefore...

P(w) + P(b) + P(r) = 1

P(r) = 1 - (P(w) + P(b))

= 1 - (0.2 + 0.3)

= 1 - 0.5

= 0.5

> ... which means that you have an even chance of picking a red sock at random.

Mutually Exclusive Outcomes

When one outcome prevents another outcome from taking place, the two outcomes are said to be MUTUALLY EXCLUSIVE. This can also be the case when there are three or more possible outcomes.

Outcomes with Equal Chances

The important rule to remember is this: 'If there are 'n' mutually exclusive outcomes, all of which are equally likely, then the probability of one outcome happening is $\frac{1}{n}$'.

Examples...

1 Tossing a coin: Here there are two mutually exclusive outcomes, Heads or Tails - if you throw a Head you can't throw a Tail!

$P(\text{Heads}) = \frac{1}{2}$
$P(\text{Tails}) = \frac{1}{2}$

Note that the probability of each outcome added together is 1, i.e. $\frac{1}{2} + \frac{1}{2} = 1$

2 Spinning a Spinner: Here there are three mutually exclusive outcomes since if you spin a red, you can't spin any other colour!

$P(\text{Red}) = \frac{1}{3}$
$P(\text{Blue}) = \frac{1}{3}$
$P(\text{Green}) = \frac{1}{3}$

Note that the probability of each outcome added together is 1, i.e. $\frac{1}{3} + \frac{1}{3} + \frac{1}{3} = 1$

3 Throwing a die: Here are six mutually exclusive outcomes, since throwing any one number prevents you from throwing the rest.

$P(\text{one}) = \frac{1}{6}$
$P(\text{two}) = \frac{1}{6}$
$P(\text{three}) = \frac{1}{6}$
$P(\text{four}) = \frac{1}{6}$
$P(\text{five}) = \frac{1}{6}$
$P(\text{six}) = \frac{1}{6}$

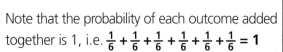

Note that the probability of each outcome added together is 1, i.e. $\frac{1}{6} + \frac{1}{6} + \frac{1}{6} + \frac{1}{6} + \frac{1}{6} + \frac{1}{6} = 1$

Outcomes with Unequal Chances

The important rule to remember is this: 'If there are 'n' mutually exclusive outcomes, but only 'a' desired outcomes, then the probability of a desired outcome is $\frac{a}{n}$'.

Examples...

1 Picking a Ball (from inside a bag): With this set of balls there are four mutually exclusive outcomes - black, green, yellow and orange. However, the chances of each colour being picked are not equal, since there are 5 blacks, 4 greens, 2 yellows and 1 orange.

$P(\text{black}) = \frac{5}{12}$
$P(\text{green}) = \frac{4}{12}$ or $\frac{1}{3}$
$P(\text{yellow}) = \frac{2}{12}$ or $\frac{1}{6}$
$P(\text{orange}) = \frac{1}{12}$

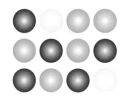

Note that the probability of each outcome added together is 1, i.e. $\frac{5}{12} + \frac{1}{3} + \frac{1}{6} + \frac{1}{12} = 1$

2 Spinning a Spinner: With this spinner there are three mutually exclusive outcomes - red, blue and green. Since the spinner has 3 reds, 2 blues and 1 green, there is an unequal chance of getting each colour.

$P(\text{red}) = \frac{3}{6}$ or $\frac{1}{2}$
$P(\text{blue}) = \frac{2}{6}$ or $\frac{1}{3}$
$P(\text{Green}) = \frac{1}{6}$

Note that the probability of each outcome added together is 1, i.e. $\frac{1}{2} + \frac{1}{3} + \frac{1}{6} = 1$

Listing all Outcomes

Outcomes of Single Events

1 **Tossing a coin.** Here there are only two outcomes: Heads or Tails

2 **Spinning a three sided spinner.** Here there are three outcomes: Red, Blue or Green

3 **Throwing a die.** Here there are only six outcomes: One, Two, Three, Four, Five or Six

In all cases like these all you have to do is make a simple list.

Outcomes of Two Successive Events

	H First coin	**T**
H	**HH**	**TH**
T	**HT**	**TT**

Second coin

1 **Tossing two coins, one after the other.**
In cases like these it is easier to use a sample space diagram to show the possible outcomes. With two coins there are 4 outcomes. The chances of each are…

$P(\text{Head} + \text{Head}) = \frac{1}{4}$
$P(\text{Tail} + \text{Tail}) = \frac{1}{4}$
$P(\text{Head} + \text{Tail}) = \frac{1}{4}$
$P(\text{Tail} + \text{Head}) = \frac{1}{4}$

Note that once again the probability of each outcome added together is 1, i.e. $\frac{1}{4} + \frac{1}{4} + \frac{1}{4} + \frac{1}{4} = 1$

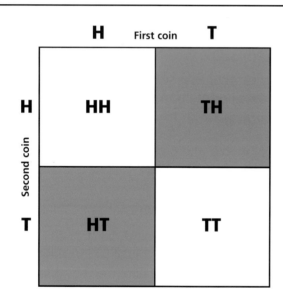

First die

	1	2	3	4	5	6
1	2	3	4	5	6	7
2	3	4	5	6	7	8
3	4	5	6	7	8	9
4	5	6	7	8	9	10
5	6	7	8	9	10	11
6	7	8	9	10	11	12

Second die

2 **Throwing a pair of dice.**
In this case, each die has six possible outcomes. The sample space diagram, which shows the scores of the two dice added together, reveals a total of 36 possible outcomes. Each outcome (e.g. throwing a 4 with the first die and a 2 with the second) has a $\frac{1}{36}$ probability.

However, while there is only a $\frac{1}{36}$ chance of scoring a total of either 2 or 12, there is a $\frac{6}{36}$ or $\frac{1}{6}$ chance of scoring a seven.

Lonsdale

Tree Diagrams

When dealing with the probability of a sequence of successive events it is better to use a tree diagram in order to simplify the task.

Example 1 - Tossing Two Coins

Again each coin can give us two possible outcomes, a HEAD (H) or a TAIL (T).

We only draw two branches as there are only two different outcomes i.e. a Head and a Tail.

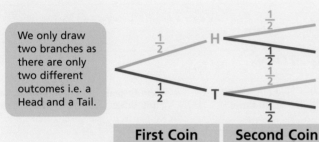

First Coin **Second Coin**

$P(HH) = P(H) \times P(H) = \frac{1}{2} \times \frac{1}{2} = \frac{1}{4}$

$P(HT) = P(H) \times P(T) = \frac{1}{2} \times \frac{1}{2} = \frac{1}{4}$

$P(TH) = P(T) \times P(H) = \frac{1}{2} \times \frac{1}{2} = \frac{1}{4}$

$P(TT) = P(T) \times P(T) = \frac{1}{2} \times \frac{1}{2} = \frac{1}{4}$

Total probability always adds up to $\boxed{1}$

Probability of getting:

1. **2 Heads, P(HH) = $\frac{1}{4}$** (should occur once)
2. **2 Tails, P(TT) = $\frac{1}{4}$** (should occur once)

3. **A Head and a Tail, P(HT) or P(TH)**
   = $\frac{1}{4} + \frac{1}{4} = \frac{1}{2}$ (should occur twice)

Example 2

From Jim's bag, the probability of selecting a red ball is 0.5, a blue ball is 0.3 and a green ball is 0.2. From Sandra's bag, the probability of selecting a red ball is 0.3, a blue ball is 0.3 and a green ball is 0.4. Jim selects a ball at random, followed by Sandra.

Draw a tree diagram to show all the different outcomes. Then calculate the probability of selecting…
1. two blues.
2. two reds or two greens.
3. different colours.

This time we draw three branches as there are three different outcomes

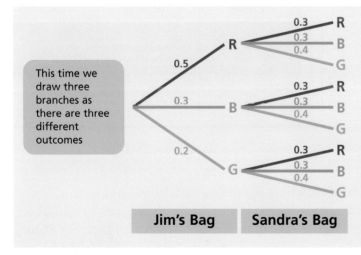

Jim's Bag **Sandra's Bag**

P (RR)	=	0.5 × 0.3	=	0.15
P (RB)	=	0.5 × 0.3	=	0.15
P (RG)	=	0.5 × 0.4	=	0.20
P (BR)	=	0.3 × 0.3	=	0.09
P (BB)	=	0.3 × 0.3	=	0.09
P (BG)	=	0.3 × 0.4	=	0.12
P (GR)	=	0.2 × 0.3	=	0.06
P (GB)	=	0.2 × 0.3	=	0.06
P (GG)	=	0.2 × 0.4	=	0.08

Total probability always adds up to $\boxed{1}$

1. **P(BB) = 0.09**
   (this outcome should occur once)
2. **P(RR) or P(GG) = 0.15 + 0.08 = 0.23**
   (this outcome should occur twice)

3. **P(different colours)**
   = P(RB), P(RG), P(BR), P(BG), P(GR), P(GB)
   = 0.15 + 0.20 + 0.09 + 0.12 + 0.06 + 0.06
   = **0.68** (this outcome should occur six times)

Relative Frequency

Theoretical Probability

Since the chance of a coin landing on Heads is $\frac{1}{2}$, then the number of Heads we should expect in 10 tosses is…

$\frac{1}{2}$ **x 10 = 5**.

This however is not always the case in reality…

Estimated Probability (Relative Frequency)

A simple experiment was carried out where a coin was tossed 10, 100 and a 1000 times. The graphs opposite show the number of Heads and Tails obtained. In our experiment we would expect to always get the same number of Heads and Tails as the probability of each event occurring is $\frac{1}{2}$ or 0.5.

The actual probability we get when we perform an experiment like this is called the RELATIVE FREQUENCY.

> **Relative Frequency =**
>
> **Number of Heads (or Tails) we get**
> **Total number of times the coin was tossed**

If we go back to our experiment, as we increase the number of times the coin is tossed, the relative frequency gets closer and closer to the theoretical probability (red dotted line), e.g. 0.5 for a Head, 0.5 for a Tail.

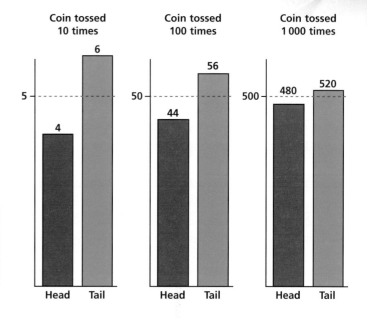

	Coin tossed 10 times	Coin tossed 100 times	Coin tossed 1 000 times
Relative Frequency	Head = $\frac{4}{10}$ = 0.4	Head = $\frac{44}{100}$ = 0.44	Head = $\frac{480}{1000}$ = 0.48
	Tail = $\frac{6}{10}$ = 0.6	Tail = $\frac{56}{100}$ = 0.56	Tail = $\frac{520}{1000}$ = 0.52

Importance of Sample Size

As you can see from the data above, the bigger the sample, the more reliable it is. It would be easy to believe that tossing a coin ten times could produce 2 tails and 8 heads!

This has implications in testing for bias. For instance it would be possible to test experimentally the frequency of red and black on a roulette wheel. If there was time to take a big enough sample then it would be possible to say with some justification that the wheel wasn't fair, e.g. if 50 000 spins produce 26 750 reds and 23 250 blacks!!

Some Definitions

- **Primary Data:** is data which has been directly obtained first hand, either by yourself or by someone under your direction. It can be collected by questionnaire, survey, observation, experiment or data logging.

- **Secondary Data:** is data which has been obtained independently by an external agency and which may be already stored either in printed or electronic form, e.g. published statistics, data from the internet.

- **The Population:** is the total number of items you are investigating.

- **The Sample:** is the limited number of items that you have selected to represent the whole population.

- **A Random Sample:** is a sample in which every item of the population has an equal chance of being selected.

Reasons for Sampling

Information is a hugely powerful tool in modern society but clearly it is impossible to survey huge populations. Sampling allows us to look at a cross-section of the population, making the process much quicker and much cheaper! Samples are used widely to inform opinion polls, market research, to produce T.V. viewing figures and to provide trend analysis.

Identifying Bias in Samples

Consider the following bad examples of sampling:

- A recent survey suggests that 82% of the population prefer Rugby League to Soccer. The survey was conducted in St Helens.

- A High Street survey reveals that 76% of men aged between 18 and 42 go to the pub at least once a week. The survey was conducted at 11pm.

- A telephone survey suggests that 100% of the population has at least one telephone in their house.

In order to be unbiased, every individual in the population must have an equal chance of being included in the sample. This means taking into account…

- The time of day of the survey
- The age range
- Relative affluence
- The geographical area
- Ethnicity
- Lifestyle

However, you must also remember that THE BIGGER THE SAMPLE SIZE, THE MORE REPRESENTATIVE IT'S LIKELY TO BE (assuming of course that you have minimised all the other potential areas of bias).

Collecting Data 2

Collecting Data by Observation

This can be laborious and time consuming but for some things it is the best way. For instance, a traffic survey might be done in this way to reveal the volume of traffic using a bridge. You must remember to ask yourself whether the survey is being conducted at and for an appropriate time.

Collecting Data by Experiment

People involved in the Sciences use experiments to gather data to support their hypotheses. The key things to remember are that the experiment must be repeated an appropriate number of times, and also that the experiment must be capable of being repeated by someone else.

Collecting Data by Questionnaire

Questionnaires are skillfully designed forms which are used to conduct surveys of a sample of the population.

Designing a Questionnaire

Good questionnaires have the following things in common…

- They are not too long. Never more than 10 questions, but less if possible.
- They contain questions which are easily understood and do not cause confusion.
- They ask for simple, short answers, e.g. Yes/No, Like/Don't Like or Male/Female
- They avoid vague words like Tall, Old, Fast, Good etc.
- The questions do not show any bias, e.g. 'Do you prefer watching rugby or hockey?' rather than, 'Do you agree that rugby is a more watchable game than hockey?'
- They only contain relevant questions.

Example

Yasmin decides to test the hypothesis that 'Parents would prefer the school holidays to be shorter' by using the following questionnaire.

This tests whether the questionnaire is relevant to this person

The answer may be affected by the size of the family!

The answer may turn out to be dependent upon the age of the person's children!

This tells us whether or not the person will see a lot of his/her children over the holidays!

This avoids asking a 'loaded question' i.e. it avoids bias

QUESTIONNAIRE

1. Do you have children of school age?
   Yes ❑ No ❑

2. How many children do you have?
   1 ❑ 2 ❑ 3 ❑ 4+ ❑

3. To which age group do they belong?
   11-13 ❑ 14-16 ❑ 17-18 ❑

4. Are you in full time employment?
   Yes ❑ No ❑

5. Do you think the school holidays are…
   Too Short? ❑
   Too Long? ❑
   Just Right? ❑

From the answers, Yasmin could…

1 Reject any responses from people who aren't parents.

2 Analyse the data to see if family size, age range and employment status affect the answers.

3 Come up with a pretty good answer to her original hypothesis.

Data comes in many different forms. To make sense of the data it is often sorted and collated. There are two different types of data that you can record for sorting and collating.

Discrete and Continuous Data

Discrete data is data that can only have certain values. For example, the number of goals a football team can score in a match is 0, 1, 2, 3, 4, etc. They cannot have a score in between, like 0.5, 1.6, 2.2, etc.

Continuous data is data that can have any value. It tends to be obtained by reading measuring instruments. The accuracy of the data is dependent on the precision of the equipment.

Tally Charts and Frequency Tables

Very often the best way to sort and collate discrete or continuous data is to draw a tally chart and a frequency table.

Example

Here are the results of the games involving Germany, the host nation, in Round 1 through to the semi-finals of the 2006 World Cup.

Germany 4 Costa Rica 2	Germany 2 Sweden 0
Germany 1 Poland 0	Germany 4 Argentina 2
Equador 0 Germany 3	Germany 0 Italy 2

Since the range of data here is narrow (e.g. from 0 to 4 goals scored) each value can be included individually in the tally chart and frequency table. As you complete the tally column always tick off each number as you go along. This makes sure that you don't include the same number twice or miss any out.

The numbers in the frequency column are simply the number of tallies. Remember to add them up, as this total is equal to the total number of pieces of data (not, in this example, the total number of goals scored!).

The data in this example is discrete, however, the same process would apply for continuous data.

Number of goals scored	Tally	Frequency of that no. of goals being scored by a team
0	IIII	4
1	I	1
2	IIII	4
3	I	1
4	II	2
		TOTAL = 12

Sorting Data 2

Using Class Intervals

Sometimes, unlike the example on the previous page, the data is so widespread that it is impractical to include each value in the tally chart and frequency table individually. When this happens, the data is sorted into groups called class intervals, where each class interval represents a range of values.

Example

The newspaper cutting shows the recorded temperatures in °C for various places both at home and abroad. Sort the recorded temperatures by drawing a tally chart and a frequency table.

Temperatures home and abroad

Amsterdam	19	Cairo	34	Majorca	27	New York	32
Athens	33	Cardiff	16	Manchester	12	Newcastle	13
Barbados	29	Dublin	15	Miami	26	Paris	20
Barcelona	26	Jersey	20	Milan	28	Peking	33
Berlin	23	London	21	Montreal	22	Prague	26
Bermuda	28	Madrid	33	Moscow	15	Rhodes	28

As you can see, the data here is widespread, e.g. from 12°C to 34°C. Out of practicality, the temperature values are arranged in groups of five in our tally chart and frequency table.

The class interval $10 \leqslant T < 15$ would include any temperature reading equal to or greater than 10°C and less than 15°C (a temperature reading of 15°C is included in the next class interval) and so on. Remember to total the numbers in the frequency column to make sure they add up to the total number of locations (pieces of data).

The data in this example is continuous, however, the same process would apply for discrete data.

Recorded temperatures, T(°C)	Tally	Frequency of temperatures falling within that range
$10 \leqslant T < 15$	||	2
$15 \leqslant T < 20$	||||	4
$20 \leqslant T < 25$	ⅢⅢ	5
$25 \leqslant T < 30$	ⅢⅢ |||	8
$30 \leqslant T < 35$	ⅢⅢ	5
		TOTAL = 24

Two Important Points

- The format of class intervals can vary. The following class intervals could have been used to give the same results for the data above: 10-14, 15-19, 20-24, etc.
- The range of each class interval depends on the total range of the data. If the total range of the data is large and the range of each class interval is small, then your frequency table would have a lot of rows. Aim to have no more than 10 lines in your table!

Lonsdale

Stem and Leaf Diagrams

A stem and leaf diagram sorts data into groups. An advantage over frequency tables is that they enable you to get more of a feel for the 'shape' of distribution. For example, the following data shows the length of time (in minutes) it took 30 pupils to complete a test, arranged in ascending order:

8, 8, 9, 15, 15, 16, 16, 17, 18, 18, 20, 21, 21, 22, 23, 26, 27, 27, 28, 28, 29, 33, 34, 34, 35, 39, 39, 42, 48, 49.

This data can be represented using a stem and leaf diagram by taking the tens to form the 'stem' of the diagram and the units to form the 'leaves'.

The end product is similar to a frequency table. However, besides allowing you to visualise the 'shape' of the data, it can be used to identify the modal class, i.e. the 20-29 group and the median (24.5 - between the 15th and 16th piece of data as there are 30 values).

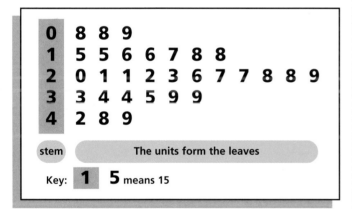

0	8 8 9
1	5 5 6 6 7 8 8
2	0 1 1 2 3 6 7 7 8 8 9
3	3 4 4 5 9 9
4	2 8 9

stem   The units form the leaves

Key: **1** **5** means 15

Two-way Tables

These simply show two sets of information, one vertically and the other horizontally. Information organised in this way can actually result in you gaining more information than you started with.

For instance, 'In a survey, 200 Year 7 and 8 pupils were asked if they preferred Maths or Science. 73 out of 110 year 7 pupils preferred Maths, and in total 82 pupils preferred Science.' This could lead to the table below:

	YEAR 7	YEAR 8	TOTAL
SCIENCE			82
MATHS	73		
TOTAL	110		200

... which in turn can be used to work out the missing data:

	YEAR 7	YEAR 8	TOTAL
SCIENCE	37	45	82
MATHS	73	45	118
TOTAL	110	90	200

Notice that in the original table there was no data for Year 8 … now it's all there!

Various Types of Table

Tables can be arranged in many different ways to suit the purpose for which they are intended. Remember, the idea is to make the information as accessible as possible, so you've got to give a bit of thought as to how you want to present it.

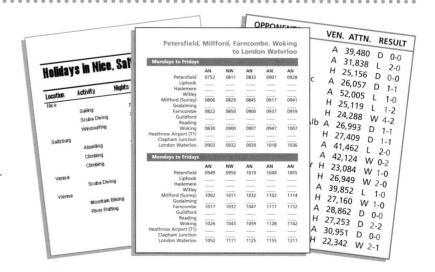

Displaying Data 1

The best way of displaying data that has been sorted into a frequency table is to draw a graph.

Here is the frequency table for the number of goals scored in games involving Germany in Round 1 through to the semi-finals of the 2006 World Cup (we only include the tally column when we are sorting the data).

No. of goals scored	Frequency
0	4
1	1
2	4
3	1
4	2

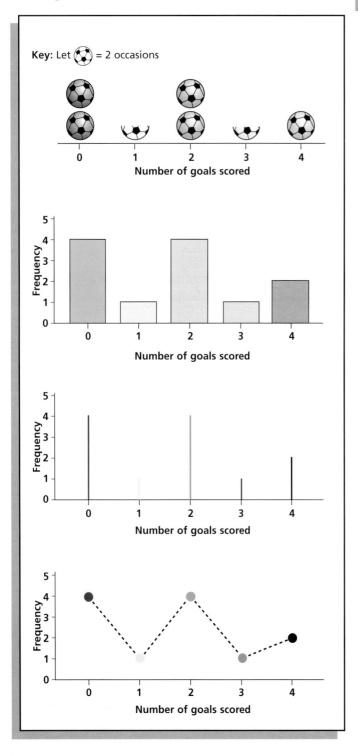

The data above can be displayed in various ways:

A Pictogram

Simple diagrams are used to display data. Since our data is about football we have used a ball. Don't forget to use the key when reading the pictogram.

A Bar Graph

Bars or columns are used to display data. Make sure that the height of each bar is equal to the correct frequency.

A Vertical Line Graph

This graph is very similar to the bar graph above, except that lines are drawn instead of bars. Make sure that the height of each line is equal to the correct frequency.

A Jagged Line Graph

This is not always the most suitable way to display discrete data, as the lines joining the points have no meaning!

Data that has been grouped together and sorted, using class intervals, in a frequency table can also be displayed by drawing a graph.

Here is the frequency table for the recorded temperatures for various locations at home and abroad.

Recorded temperatures T(°C)	Frequency
$10 \leqslant T < 15$	2
$15 \leqslant T < 20$	4
$20 \leqslant T < 25$	5
$25 \leqslant T < 30$	8
$30 \leqslant T < 35$	5

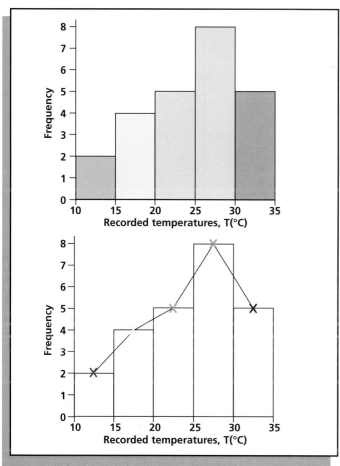

The data above can be displayed in various ways:

A Frequency Diagram

This is very much like a bar graph, but since we have grouped data then the bars do not have a gap between them, i.e. they must be continuous, one after another.

A Frequency Polygon

All you need to do is mark the middle of the top of each bar in the frequency diagram with a cross and then join up these crosses with straight lines.

You may be asked to draw a frequency polygon directly from the frequency table. You must remember to plot the crosses at the correct frequency exactly over the middle of the class intervals, e.g. for **$10 \leqslant T < 15$**, plot the cross above 12.5

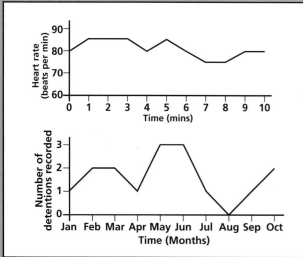

Time Series

One of the most frequently used forms of displaying continuous data involves plotting a line graph of a particular variable against time. This is called a time series. Examples could include:

- The noon temperature in your garden every Sunday
- The daily value of the FTSE 100
- Your height at yearly intervals
- A hardware shop's monthly sales

REMEMBER! In time series graphs, 'Time' is always on the **x**-axis (horizontal).

Scatter Diagrams 1

A scatter diagram is a graph which has two sets of data plotted on it at the same time. When plotted the points may show a certain trend or correlation. A correlation is defined as the 'strength of relationship between two variables'.

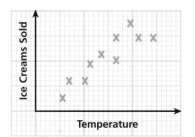

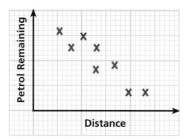

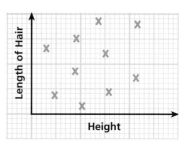

Positive Correlation

As one increases, the other also increases, e.g. number of ice creams sold and daytime temperature.

Negative Correlation

As one increases, the other decreases or vice-versa, e.g. amount of petrol left in tank and distance travelled by car.

Zero Correlation

No obvious trend between the two, e.g. length of hair and height. Remember that zero correlation does not necessarily imply 'no relationship' but merely 'no linear relationship'

Line of Best Fit

This is a straight line that passes through the points so that we have as many points above the line as we have below the line. A line of best fit can only be drawn if our points show positive or negative correlation. Opposite are four different examples of lines of best fit.

A and **B** are **POOR** lines of best fit. They both have the same number of points above and below the line but these points are bunched together and not spread out.

C and **D** are **GOOD** lines of best fit. They both have the same number of points above and below the lines and these points are spread out.

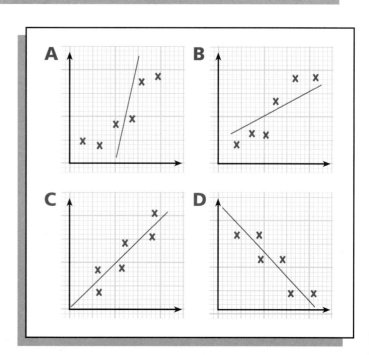

Lonsdale

Scatter Diagrams 2

Example

Maths mark	60	30	46	89	48	78	26	38	91	20	65	73
Science mark	56	30	47	98	61	77	38	51	89	25	80	87

The table gives the maths mark and science mark for 12 pupils in their end of year examinations.

a) Draw a scatter diagram, including a line of best fit, to show the marks.

b) Tim was absent from his science exam but he achieved a mark of 65 in his maths exam. Use your graph to work out an estimated science mark for Tim.

c) Jenny achieved a mark of 42 in her science exam but she was absent for her maths exam. Again use your graph to work out an estimated maths mark for Jenny.

Solution

a)

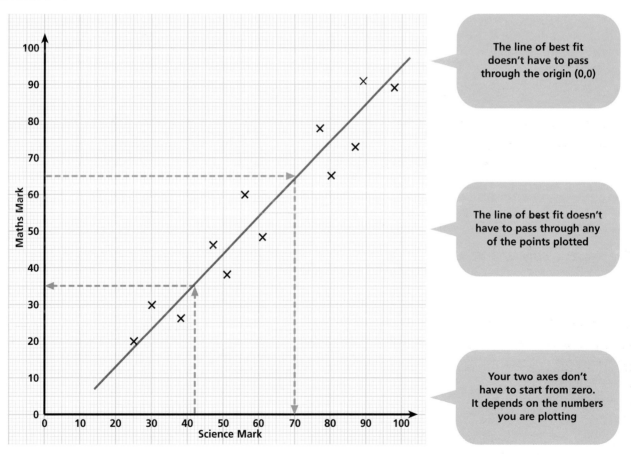

The line of best fit doesn't have to pass through the origin (0,0)

The line of best fit doesn't have to pass through any of the points plotted

Your two axes don't have to start from zero. It depends on the numbers you are plotting

b) Go to 65 on the maths axis and then draw a dotted line ACROSS TO (→) the LINE OF BEST FIT and then DOWN TO (↓) the science axis. This is Tim's estimated science mark.

Answer is 70

c) Go to 42 on the science axis and then draw a dotted line UP TO (↑) the LINE OF BEST FIT and then ACROSS TO (←) the maths axis. This is Jenny's estimated maths mark.

Answer is 35

Pie Charts

Drawing Pie Charts

Another way of displaying sorted data is to draw a pie chart. A pie chart is a circle which is split into different sectors. Here are the results of a survey carried out among 18 pupils to find their favourite sport.

Before we can draw our pie chart we need to calculate the ANGLE of the sector representing each sport. To do this we work out the fraction of the pupils for each sport, then multiply this fraction by 360°.

We can now draw our pie chart. Always measure all angles carefully with a protractor and make sure that you always use the scale on your protractor that starts at 0°.

Favourite Sport	Frequency (no. of pupils)
Football	7
Tennis	3
Hockey	8
	Total = 18

Favourite Sport	Frequency of pupils	Angle to be drawn
Football	Total number of pupils → $\frac{7}{18}$ ← Number who liked football	$\frac{7}{18}$ x 360° = 140°
Tennis	Total number of pupils → $\frac{3}{18}$ ← Number who liked Tennis	$\frac{3}{18}$ x 360° = 60°
Hockey	Total number of pupils → $\frac{8}{18}$ ← Number who liked Hockey	$\frac{8}{18}$ x 360° = 160°
		Total = 360°

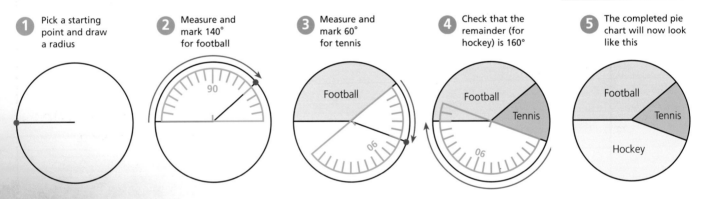

① Pick a starting point and draw a radius

② Measure and mark 140° for football

③ Measure and mark 60° for tennis

④ Check that the remainder (for hockey) is 160°

⑤ The completed pie chart will now look like this

Getting Information from Pie Charts

Getting information from a pie chart is very similar to drawing a pie chart except you need to work backwards. If the pie chart above shows the favourite sport for 18 pupils, the first thing we need to do is measure all the angles. We can then work out the number of pupils for each sport.

Favourite Sport	Fraction of circle	Number of pupils
Football	Total no. of ° for a circle → $\frac{140°}{360°}$ ← Number of ° for football	$\frac{140°}{360°}$ x 18 = 7
Tennis	Total no. of ° for a circle → $\frac{60°}{360°}$ ← Number of ° for tennis	$\frac{60°}{360°}$ x 18 = 3
Hockey	Total no. of ° for a circle → $\frac{160°}{360°}$ ← Number of ° for hockey	$\frac{160°}{360°}$ x 18 = 8
		Total = 18 pupils

Mean, Median, Mode & Range 1

Describing Data

We often use the word 'average' to describe a set of data and this is quite a useful tool. However, two batsmen who both average 35 in five innings could have had the following scores, showing quite different distributions:

Batsman A: 0, 10, 10, 60, 95
Batsman B: 30, 34, 36, 36, 39

In this case the 'average' score doesn't tell us the whole story. For this, we can use three different types of average, **mean**, **median** and **mode**, plus a description of the **range** of the data.

Example

Sam has the following coins in his pocket. What he has is a distribution of numbers (the different valued coins).

① Mean

This is the AVERAGE value and is given by:

$$\text{Mean} = \frac{\textbf{SUM OF ALL THE VALUES}}{\textbf{NUMBER OF VALUES}}$$

$$= \frac{1p+5p+1p+20p+10p+5p+1p+1p+10p}{9 \text{ (number of coins)}}$$

$$= \frac{54p}{9} = \textbf{6p}$$

② Median

This is the MIDDLE value, providing that all the numbers have been arranged in order, lowest to highest.

1p, 1p, 1p, 1p, 5p, 5p, 10p, 10p, 20p `Arrange in order`

1̶p̶, 1̶p̶, 1̶p̶, 1̶p̶, 5p, 5̶p̶, 1̶0̶p̶, 1̶0̶p̶, 2̶0̶p̶ `Tick off from the two ends to find the middle value`

Median = 5p

If you tick off from the two ends and are left with two numbers in the middle, then the median is the number halfway between those two numbers (e.g. for 1̶, 1̶, 1, 2, 2̶, 2̶ **Median = 1.5**)

③ Mode

This is the MOST COMMON value, i.e. the number that occurs most frequently.

Mode = 1p `1p coin occurs more times than any other coin`

④ Range

This is the DIFFERENCE between the HIGHEST and the LOWEST value.

Range = 20p - 1p **= 19p**

Mean, Median, Mode & Range 2

Mean, Median, Mode and Range from a Frequency Table

Here is the frequency table (again) for the number of goals scored in games involving Germany from round 1 through to the semi-finals of the 2006 World Cup.

The data in this frequency table is discrete. The same processes would apply if the data was continuous.

Number of goals scored (x)	Frequency (f)	Frequency x no. of goals scored (fx)	
0	4	4 x 0 = 0	4 teams have scored 0 goals. Total number of goals scored = 4 x 0 = 0
1	1	1 x 1 = 1	1 team has scored 1 goal. Total number of goals scored = 1 x 1 = 1
2	4	4 x 2 = 8	4 teams have scored 2 goals. Total number of goals scored = 4 x 2 = 8
3	1	1 x 3 = 3	1 team has scored 3 goals. Total number of goals scored = 1 x 3 = 3
4	2	2 x 4 = 8	2 teams have scored 4 goals. Total number of goals scored = 2 x 4 = 8
	Total = 12	Total = 20	Total number of goals scored. = 0 + 1 + 8 + 3 + 8 = 20

Mean

To calculate the mean we need to add another column (in red) to our frequency table to calculate the total number of goals scored.

$$\text{Mean} = \frac{\text{Total number of goals scored (fx)}}{\text{Total frequency}}$$

$$= \frac{20}{12} = 1.\dot{6} \text{ goals (per team per game)}$$

Mode

Mode = 0 goals and 2 goals

(these occur more times than any of the others).

NOTE: You may well be asked to identify the modal class from a frequency table involving grouped data (see example on page 106). In the stated example the modal class is **25°C<T<30°C** since this class interval has the highest frequency (i.e. it occurs the most number of times).

Median

Since we have 12 pieces of data, the median number of goals is halfway between the 6th and 7th piece of data (with an even number you always end up with two numbers in the middle).

4 teams scored	1 team scored	4 teams scored	1 team scored	2 teams scored
0̶ 0̶ 0̶ 0̶	1̶	②②2̶ 2̶	3̶	4̶4̶

$$\text{Median} = \frac{2 + 2}{2}$$
$$= 2 \text{ goals}$$

Range

Range = 4 goals - 0 goals
$$= 4 \text{ goals}$$

Lonsdale

Mean, Median, Mode & Range 3

Mean, Median and Mode from a Frequency Table Involving Grouped Data

Here is the frequency table for the recorded temperatures for various locations at home and abroad.

The data in this frequency table is continuous. The same processes would apply if the data was discrete.

Recorded temperatures, T (°C)	Frequency (f)	mid-temp. values (x)	Frequency x mid-temp. values (fx)
10 ≤ T < 15	2	12.5	2 x 12.5 = 25
15 ≤ T < 20	4	17.5	4 x 17.5 = 70
20 ≤ T < 25	5	22.5	5 x 22.5 = 112.5
25 ≤ T < 30	8	27.5	8 x 27.5 = 220
30 ≤ T < 35	5	32.5	5 x 32.5 = 162.5
	Total = 24		Total = 590

These are class intervals

These are halfway values for our class intervals

Estimated Mean

With grouped data, the individual values are unknown. Therefore we have to use 'mid-temperature value' to provide an **estimate** of the mean. To calculate the mean this time we need to add two further columns (in red) to our frequency table.

$$\text{Mean} = \frac{\text{Total of recorded temperatures (f}x\text{)}}{\text{Total frequency}}$$

$$= \frac{590}{24}$$

$$= 24.58°C$$

Mode

Again we don't get an exact mode but we are able to determine which class interval or group is the MODAL CLASS. Modal Class is **25°C ≤ T < 30°C** since this class interval has the highest frequency (i.e. it occurs the most number of times).

Median

With continuous data we don't get an exact value for the median, but we are able to determine which class interval or group it is in. The above table has 24 pieces of data and so the median is halfway between the 12th and 13th piece of data. Using the frequency column, the median is in the **25°C ≤ T < 30°C** class interval.

Lonsdale

Using a Scientific Calculator 1

Exam Preparation

The Day Before the Exam…
- Check that your calculator is working properly.

Before Entering the Exam…
- Check that your calculator screen is clear.
- Check that the MEMORY is clear.
- Make sure that any FIX, SCI or ENG functions, which may affect your calculations, have been switched off.
- Many calculators have a RESET button on the back. It is a good idea to press this before the exam to restore the basic settings.

*Please note that some calculators may have different operating methods. Please check your own against the examples given.

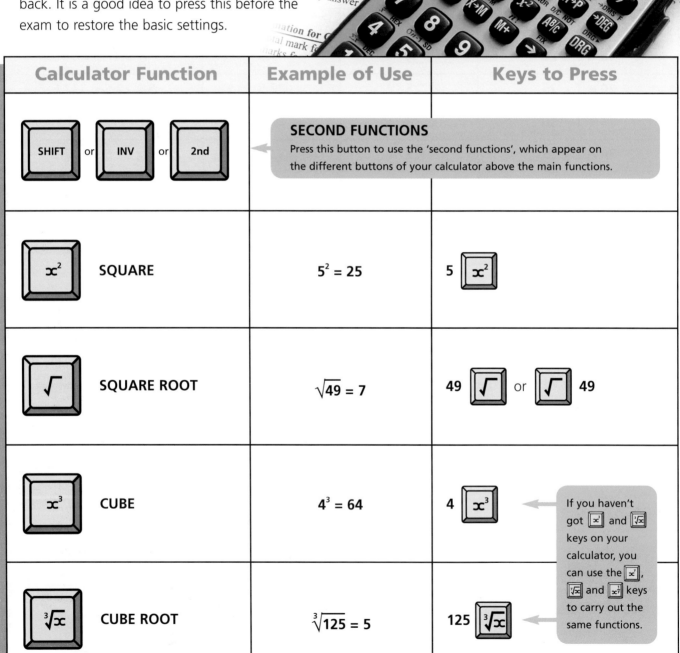

Calculator Function	Example of Use	Keys to Press
SHIFT or **INV** or **2nd**	**SECOND FUNCTIONS** Press this button to use the 'second functions', which appear on the different buttons of your calculator above the main functions.	
x^2 SQUARE	$5^2 = 25$	5 x^2
$\sqrt{}$ SQUARE ROOT	$\sqrt{49} = 7$	49 $\sqrt{}$ or $\sqrt{}$ 49
x^3 CUBE	$4^3 = 64$	4 x^3
$\sqrt[3]{x}$ CUBE ROOT	$\sqrt[3]{125} = 5$	125 $\sqrt[3]{x}$

If you haven't got x^y and $\sqrt[x]{x}$ keys on your calculator, you can use the x^y, $\sqrt[x]{x}$ and $x^{\frac{1}{y}}$ keys to carry out the same functions.

Lonsdale

Using a Scientific Calculator 2

Calculator Function	Example of Use	Keys to Press
x^y POWER	$4^6 = 4096$	4 x^y 6
$x^{\frac{1}{y}}$ or $\sqrt[y]{x}$ ROOT	$\sqrt[4]{6561} = 9$	6561 $x^{\frac{1}{y}}$ 4 or 4 $x^{\frac{1}{y}}$ 6561
Min MR MEMORY	Finally get used to using the memory buttons. Min stores a number (usually the answer to a calculation) in the calculator's memory. MR is used to recall the number when needed e.g. as part of a related calculation.	
$a\frac{b}{c}$ FRACTION	To key in $2\frac{3}{5}$	2 $a\frac{b}{c}$ 3 $a\frac{b}{c}$ 5
$\frac{d}{c}$	Press $\frac{d}{c}$ to convert keyed-in mixed number into an improper fraction. Press $a\frac{b}{c}$ again to convert improper fraction into a decimal.	
[(... ...)] BRACKETS	$(5 + 2) \times 6 = 42$	[(... 5 + 2 ...)] x 6 =
EXP EE STANDARD FORM	To key in 5.2×10^6	5.2 EXP 6

Formulae Sheet

These are the formulae issued by Edexcel for foundation tier students.

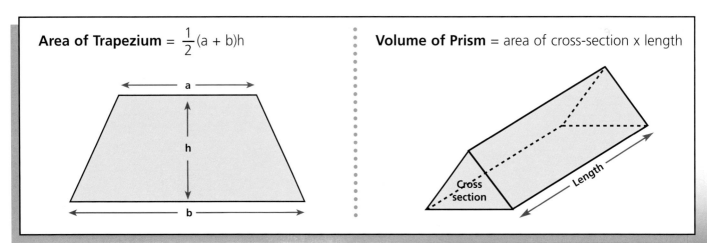

Area of Trapezium = $\frac{1}{2}(a + b)h$

Volume of Prism = area of cross-section x length

Index 2